Praise for *Finding Joy*

"Dewey Williams, pastor and chaplain...
taken us with him on an amazing journey...
open to the domain of true joy. Carrying us with him as he ministers
to men and women on Death Row—and even to painful places in his
own sojourn—he offers testimony to contradict the misconception
that joy is found only when life is on terms we set. With skillful pen,
he shows that the Lord Jesus can give joy under dire circumstances.
Take the journey with him and you will not regret it, to say the least."
— William Turner Jr., PhD, James T. and Alice
Mead Cleland professor emeritus of the Practice
of Preaching at Duke Divinity School

"This book is a beautiful integration of stories demonstrating what
is possible in impossible circumstances. Where there is great sorrow,
there can also be great joy. Where there is suffering, there can also be
love. Where there is death, there can also be life."
— Angela Williams Gorrell, author of *The Gravity
of Joy: A Story of Being Lost and Found*

"In *Finding Joy on Death Row*, Pastor Dewey Williams has accom-
plished a rare feat: He has simultaneously inspired joy through his
compassionate sermons for and meaningful presence with the persons
living on Death Row, elevated joy in his readers who may more easily
than expected see themselves in these narratives, and rediscovered
joy many times over in his own vocational and personal paths. With
great humility and transparency, this author conveys the depth of his
own triumphs and tragedies, even as their occurrences run parallel to
those of the Death Row population he serves. In the face of systemic
inequalities in the criminal justice system and painful circumstances
for all involved, he nonetheless elevates the reader's attention to the
experience of joy on Death Row and, even more importantly, the
Source of their joy. Author, women and men on Death Row, and

reader alike are united in their recognition that not only incarceration imprisons: loss, addictions, mental health issues, and alienation can contribute to rage, stagnancy, unforgiveness, and other forms of despair in the midnight hour. Still, we learn with increasing certainty that joy is God's work and God's business, and we are privileged as we learn to enjoy God's fruit. Indeed, this compelling and hopeful work confirms that in God's presence is fullness of joy."

—Dr. Tonya D. Armstrong, licensed psychologist, CEO of the Armstrong Center for Hope, associate minister, and author/producer of *Blossoming Hope: The Black Christian Woman's Guide to Mental Health and Wellness* and *Blossoming Hope Companion: Soothing Songs and Spoken Word Recordings*

"Dewey Williams describes how for decades he lived a defeated life, devoid of joy. He lost his joy as a young man in a traumatic and tragic event that took the life of his father and the soul of his sister. He found joy on Death Row among people who had taken the lives of others. As the psalmist reminds us, 'Weeping may linger for the night, but joy comes with the morning' (Psalm 30:5). Read this book and find your joy."

—Curtis W. Freeman, research professor of theology and director of the Baptist House of Studies at Duke Divinity School

"*Finding Joy on Death Row* is filled with intimate narrative from Dewey Williams and illuminating testimonies of women and men on North Carolina's Death Row that offer a tender and transparent text that will transform you."

—David Emmanuel Goatley, PhD, President of Fuller Theological Seminary

"Dewey Williams and I share a pair of academic institutions: Yale Divinity School and Duke Divinity School. But Dewey has introduced me to a locale where I have never been and can't see myself ever going. I'm talking about Death Row in a North Carolina prison. His description is so real, I can hear the bars clink as the gates close behind me. And his depiction of the inmates involved is so vivid that I can feel them come alive as he tells their stories and allows me to read their writings. But it is his story that is so raw and real, so personal and powerful, that kept me turning pages as I read his autobiographical remembrances. His book is a wonderful marriage of memoir and ministry. I wish that I could have him in class one more time."

—William Ritter, retired United Methodist
minister and former visiting professor of
homiletics at Duke Divinity School

FINDING

JOY

ON

DEATH ROW

Foreword by Rev. Dr. Braxton D. Shelley
Associate Professor of Music and Divinity, Yale Divinity School

FINDING
JOY
ON
DEATH ROW

UNEXPECTED LESSONS
FROM LIVES WE DISCARDED

DEWEY WILLIAMS

DEXTERITY
NASHVILLE

604 Magnolia Lane
Nashville, TN 37211

Unless otherwise noted, Scripture quotations are taken from the New Revised
Standard Version, Updated Edition. Copyright © 2021 National Council of
Churches of Christ in the United States of America. Used by permission. All
rights reserved worldwide.

Scripture quotations marked NLT are taken from the *Holy Bible*, New Living
Translation, copyright © 1996, 2004, 2015 by Tyndale House Foundation. Used by
permission of Tyndale House Publishers, Carol Stream, Illinois 60188. All rights
reserved.

Scripture quotations marked KJV are taken from the King James Version. Public
domain.

Inmate stories used with permissions. Some names have been changed or initials
used instead of full names, on request.

Printed in the United States of America.

First edition: 2023
10 9 8 7 6 5 4 3 2 1

ISBN: 978-1-947297-55-5 (Paperback)
ISBN: 978-1-947297-56-2 (E-book)

Publisher's Cataloging-in-Publication Data
Names: Williams, Charles Dewey, author.
Title: Finding joy on death row : unexpected lessons from lives we discarded /
Dewey Williams.
Description: Includes bibliographical references. | Nashville, TN: Dexterity
Collective, 2023.
Identifiers: ISBN: 978-1-947297-55-5 (paperback) | 978-1-947297-56-2 (ebook)
Subjects: LCSH Death row inmates--United States. | Capital punishment--
United States. | Prisoners--
Religious life. | Church work with prisoners--United States. | BISAC RELIGION
/ Christian Ministry /
General | SOCIAL SCIENCE / Capital Punishment
Classification: LCC BV4340 .W55 2023 | DDC 259/.5--dc23

Cover design by Kieron Lewis and Sarah Siegand
Interior design by PerfecType, Nashville, TN

To my father, Granville Manuel Williams Sr.
I wish I was half the man you were.

Though the fig tree does not blossom
and no fruit is on the vines;
though the produce of the olive fails
and the fields yield no food;
though the flock is cut off from the fold
and there is no herd in the stalls,
yet I will rejoice in the LORD;
I will exult in the God of my salvation.

Habakkuk 3:17–18

CONTENTS

Foreword by Braxton D. Shelley   xv

Introduction   Joy Amid Tragedy   1

CHAPTER 1   The Mystery of Joy   7

CHAPTER 2   Joy Refreshes and Renews   11

CHAPTER 3   Unexpected Joy   19

CHAPTER 4   Joy Is God's Work   31

CHAPTER 5   Seeing Joy Clearly   47

CHAPTER 6   Joy in Lockup?   59

CHAPTER 7   Anger and Joy   81

CHAPTER 8   The Crippling of My Joy   89

CHAPTER 9   Late-Night Joy   109

CHAPTER 10   Joy with Shortages   127

CHAPTER 11   Joy Grows Dim   145

CHAPTER 12   Joy in Community   151

CHAPTER 13   Selfishness and Joy   163

CHAPTER 14   Joy Overshadowed   175

CHAPTER 15   Joy Within   183

CHAPTER 16   Separation and Joy   195

CHAPTER 17 Joy Takes Root   211

CHAPTER 18 Joy Shared   223

CHAPTER 19 Joy Blossoms   239

CHAPTER 20 Joyous Reunion   247

Resources   271

Acknowledgments   273

Notes   277

About the Author   281

FOREWORD

Entering a prison, for those incarcerated and visitors alike, is an exercise is undressing. The customary removal of devices and instruments that could threaten the operation of life behind bars means that the bodies that gain access to the inner courts of a penal institution weigh far less than they did when they arrived on the premises. Stripped down of items that were important enough to carry, but not safe enough to keep, the souls who move around a prison are all too conscious that the life unfolding on the inside is something different from what transpires on the outside. Each prison is an "other space," which is Michel Foucault's phrase for places that stand outside the everyday, exposing the constructedness and arbitrariness of the things we take for granted. Who would have thought that an "other space," the inside of the inside, Unit 3 of North Carolina's Central Prison, would give a sad preacher a place to break free? This unlikely story is what unfolds in the pages of Reverend Dewey Williams's *Finding Joy on Death Row: Unexpected Lessons from Lives We Discarded.*

We sing about it. We preach about it. We talk about it. But what is joy? My tradition teaches that joy is not happiness. It is not dependent on circumstances. It is that which comes after nights of weeping. Joy: the joy of the Lord. This joy is our strength. Although joy is something that can be talked about in the abstract, it can only be lived out concretely. Joy shows up. Joy invades. Joy can be found in unpredictable places. When Reverend Williams recounts the transformative effects of his visits to Death Row, he outlines a journey into joy, a story that began decades ago and continues into the present. This journey has carried Reverend Williams through Iowa, Texas, Colorado, and North Carolina, through Duke Divinity School, Yale Divinity School, Durham's Guess Road Prison, and Raleigh's Central Prison. On one occasion in December 2016, I was privileged to witness Reverend Dewey lead those imprisoned in song and in sermon, preaching to them about the joy that the angel brought to shepherds with the announcement of Jesus's birth. As he shared the good news first given to ancient outcasts with those locked away from contemporary society, a palpable and improbable presence of joy arose on Death Row. That joy could appear when least expected reveals something important about joy itself. As Reverend Williams explains, Christian joy depends "not on events, but on God's work" in a person's life. And this divine work can greet one in surprising encounters.

The close relationships that emerged between Reverend Dewey and those to whom he ministered leap from the pages of this book. This rapport crossed divisions that are often treated as impermeable. One of the things I love most about this book is the responsible and respectful way that the voices of the incarcerated are woven into the discussion. Their thoughts, their ideas, their understandings of the kinds of joy that are available to them—even, and especially, in the heart of Central Prison—are essential to the story Reverend Dewey tells. And there is much profundity in what Reverend Dewey's interlocutors have to say. I will never forget the first time Dewey told me about the locked-away man who changed the name of his habitation, claiming that instead of "Death Row," he now lives on "Life Row."

Returning to these words in the context of this excellent book clarifies the deep wisdom of these words, one that resides in the substitution of life for death. He is right to claim that despite the name of his assigned section of the penitentiary, the death sentence that will end his life will not necessarily be the final word about his life. For as long as he lives, he will *just* live. He will *so* live.

In this way, those who are not imprisoned have much in common with this incarcerated sage. For as much as he is on "Life Row," the rest of us are all assembled on something that might be analogized to "Death Row." Now, in saying this, I do not mean to make light of the terrible predicament into which so many have been placed—by criminal actions, by unjust laws, and by prosecutorial deceit. Nor do I intend to distract from efforts aimed at abolishing the state's right to end any human life. What I am after here is the sense in which all those who live are perpetually surrounded by death. This book speaks to the reality that all life is lived in the face of death. We are buffeted by mortality, battered by loss, grappling with grief. We must deal with disappointment, addiction, anxiety, fear, and heartache. These are obstacles to joy. But they are not insurmountable. This is the lesson of *Finding Joy on Death Row*: a reminder that joy is a pursuit, a path, and a process. No one can preach this sermon like Reverend Dewey, for he is well acquainted with joy's opponents. In this text, Pastor Williams honestly discloses the traumas and losses, the disappointments and detours that threatened to hide joy from him. At the same time, he enlightens us that it was not in some grand cathedral that joy was resurrected. Nor did his joy arise from a comparative pity for those to whom he ministered. Reverend Dewey found joy on Death Row through recognition—literally, re-cognition: thinking anew about the circumstances with which he had been faced, finding that he, too, lived on "Life Row."

Given its concern with the perennial question of how to live in the face of death, this book is both timely and eternal. Perhaps it can be called "eternally timely." Above all, *Finding Joy on Death Row* is highly convicting. It leaves the reader with an awesome question: If joy can be found on Death Row, then why not in every other place?

Rev. Dr. Braxton D. Shelley
Associate Professor of Music and Divinity, Yale Divinity School

INTRODUCTION

Joy Amid Tragedy

In October 2016, I found myself in conversation with a man sentenced to die. He was on North Carolina's Death Row for shooting and killing his girlfriend at point-blank range with their infant son in bed at her side. Though I had seemingly wandered into the Death Row preaching assignment by chance, this brief conversation changed my life.

I was ripe for the picking. The person assigned the rare opportunity to preach at Central Prison could no longer come on Sundays. Then the man scheduled to preach the annual Christmas sermon canceled too. It was a straightforward assignment: a monthly time set aside to lead worship and a one-time Christmas service.

Why me? First, I was authorized as a volunteer, and the lead chaplain knew me. I had already jumped through the North Carolina Department of Correction's security hoops and accompanied other volunteers at Raleigh's maximum-security prison. Second, I was able to bring prayer and meditation to those who self-identified as Christians. At sixty years old, I had recently completed my divinity degree at Duke University, a degree I had started more than four decades earlier. Most important, my schedule was open. My heart longed to pastor a local congregation, but frustrating as it was to me, I was not pastoring at the time.

My attitude at the inception of the experience I share within these pages reminds me of my elementary school self: a boy who needed glasses but didn't realize the severity of his handicap until he put on his first pair of prescription eyewear. The chaplain's invitation to share faith with men sentenced to death came at a point in my life when I was ready to give up on ministry. And here, as I faced my hopelessness, I got a chance to preach. Looking back, I understand it as an invitation for me to journey forward in my own life.

Back then, I was secretly locked up in my own prison—one created *for* me and *by* me. Bullying, prejudice, and poverty in my youth in Iowa and Colorado had laid the prison's foundation. Then walls grew up around me when a traumatic, life-altering event scattered my family across the country, disconnecting us from one another and everything we knew. The roof of my prison was constructed when my vocational dream to pastor did not materialize as I had hoped. Then the doors locked me in when I lost my oldest daughter. No matter how far I had come as a person, no matter how distant I was geographically from how and where I was raised, and no matter what façade I put on, I could not escape hopelessness.

Aren't men and women of the cloth better prepared with spiritual armor to weather such storms? In my case, no. Then joy raised its head in my life in a very powerful way.

In 2016, in advance of my Death Row invitation, I was determined to find how joy plays out in life. In researching joy, I discovered a preaching competition at Yale Divinity School's Center for Faith & Culture. The competition—part of a larger program titled the Theology of Joy and the Good Life—invited sermon submissions responding to questions concerning joy and flourishing. Pastors and seminarians from sixty locations in twenty-seven states and five countries participated. I was motivated to do a good job, but I also felt like a farce. Who was I, in my hopeless state, to teach people sentenced to die about joy? Would a preeminent divinity school even consider my submission?

Prison ministry takes a certain type of person. Not all preachers find themselves with the opportunity or the time or the inclination. Many purposely avoid serving those who are incarcerated. And for good reason. It's tough work. It can be scary, guilt inducing, and frustrating. There is zero compensation to serve. People who give their time in service to those locked away—many who attest to their innocence and others who endure extremely harsh sentences—are genuine, concerned missionaries who must struggle with one of the most complicated and emotional issues in society: criminal justice.

As you might imagine, if ministering in prison is one thing, doing so on Death Row is a whole new level. Most on Death Row are condemned for committing a combination of heinous crimes: murder and armed robbery, murder and rape, or murder and kidnapping. All on Death Row, guilty or not, are labeled as throwaway people deserving of the harshest retribution, beyond saving in the eyes of society. I had no inkling of how many of the nearly 150 people on North Carolina's Death Row would be open to my words of joy.

Nevertheless, I plodded on. I planned five sermons on joy. On my first day visiting Death Row, the walls of my personal prison started to crumble. The aforementioned man convicted of shooting and killing his girlfriend with their infant son in bed at her side sat beside me during a break. As we snacked on refreshments, he shocked me when he said triumphantly, "I have decided that I am not on 'Death

Row.' I am on 'Life Row,' and I am going to live my life every day the best way I can." This man had been in prison for almost twenty-five years. As time allowed his message to percolate within me, it ultimately motivated me. Perhaps we could share joy in this desolate place! Perhaps everyone, everywhere, no matter whether their prison was real or imagined, could find joy.

As the preaching experience continued, my cage unlocked, and I sought to know my audience more deeply. We created small groups to discuss the sermons and the Bible, and I asked the incarcerated men to respond to the ideas in writing.

I found I played a unique role in a couple of ways. Most of the volunteers are White. Most of the people who are incarcerated are Black. Being African American not only allowed me a natural trust relationship with the imprisoned but also made me an expert on Black churches and culture when the White volunteers were often stumped by a question or reaction. I also had a useful, authentic technique. Through years in the church, in training, and as a social worker, I learned to teach the group I worked with—a dysfunctional family, a Bible study class, a group of incarcerated people—how they are the authorities of their own experiences. They know their lives, their situations, their hopes. I was merely there to listen and help. My unique role and technique allowed an opening up—a bridge between worlds—that encouraged those locked up to share their stories.

In the following pages, you will read the written responses to the sermons along with many heartbreaking personal stories of wrongdoing and redemption, guilt and innocence, and choices made with and without faith. I will also share how I confronted my demons in a world of despair and, ultimately, won the prize from Yale Divinity School.

Each one of us has had times when life pushed us down; when we made decisions we regret; when we faced unexpected, unfortunate circumstances; when we struggled against hopelessness. By examining the struggle, we can find the kind of joy that works against that hopelessness. We are all children of God, and—no matter the dastardly deeds committed or the misfortune bestowed—when we engage and listen, we receive.

This book is for criminals and victims and anyone locked up in prison, real or imagined. You will find in the words of the incarcerated a great deal of sorrow, regret, abandonment, and anger. You will likewise find humility, hope, love, perseverance, forgiveness, and deep faith. It is not for me or you to judge these responses. Instead, I attest we can learn from them. To the victims of crime, especially the family members who are victims of those on Death Row, I care about you and want the best for you. The path forward is difficult, but I believe what I offer in this book welcomes you to find joy like these souls on Death Row have found joy and like I've found joy after my losses. I offer more than prayers and more than prisons. I offer a doorway to joy that is opened to you now.

This book is for those who choose to follow Jesus and those who do not. I am not sharing these stories to convince you that you must follow God and the teachings of Jesus Christ to find joy in your life. Instead, I wish to illustrate how joy changed the lives of people with the dimmest of outlooks and how their outpouring of joy changed me. I found joy on Death Row. If such transformation can happen to me, it can happen to you.

ONE

The Mystery of Joy

I'll never forget my first time on Death Row. The doorway was about six feet wide with metal bars about four inches thick. The noise the door made when it opened and closed sounded like metal being pushed and pulled on a metal track inside the walls. The walls were about twelve inches thick, fortified with concrete. The door took seven or eight seconds to completely open or close. The door closed with a metallic clank of the lock, letting me know I was secured inside. I went through three of these doors *before* the initial screening area of the prison. A correctional officer stood behind an expansive glass area, controlling the metal doors and only allowing for one of the three doors to be open at a time. If the wrong person managed to get past one door, they would need to get past two more to get in or out of prison.

Early on I learned that these gatekeepers were not to be messed with. They could be detrimental to the access I needed. I learned that correctional officers, too, are incarcerated while they work, and they would seek to show signs of power and control whenever they felt crossed. In subsequent years I realized that the incarcerated would attempt to show their power and control whenever they could.

After I was ushered through the security door and it closed behind me, I was in a square room, about twenty feet by twenty feet. Here, correctional officers patted down everyone going into the prison. This prevented someone outside from bringing in contraband that had passed through the metal detector. Anything that was not supposed to be brought into prison would be found in this step, or so they hoped. Further, any person coming in and out of prison had to carry transparent bags. All the correctional officers and staff went through these same doors and procedures.

I emptied my pockets and turned them inside out to show that nothing was in them. Then I took off my jacket and handed it to the officer so he could look through my jacket pockets. The only items I had brought were my driver's license, my prison volunteer card, and my keys, and I placed them in a small bin while I was patted down.

Some people were entering the prison like me, and others waited to exit. The three doors created two waiting areas that moved people in and out. People waiting to exit stood in a line, and people waiting to enter stood in a separate line on the opposite side. Since none of the three doors could be open simultaneously, we all found ourselves waiting to move forward.

Soon the chaplain met me, and we headed down a long hallway. We had not seen each other for two months, and her church singing group had just done a performance at Carnegie Hall. We spent much of our walk to Death Row talking about her trip to New York. At the dead end of this hallway was a bank of vending machines selling soft drinks and snacks, and around the corner were two elevators. The elevators had no call button; instead, a person on the other side of a camera controlled the elevators and sent an elevator to the correct floor. Once the elevator opened, the chaplain held up two fingers as a signal to the elevator operator.

Once on the third floor, we made the long walk up an inclined corridor. The expansive walkway had sets of electronic locking doors, one on each side of the walkway. Someone controlled these electronic security doors. About halfway up on the left, we arrived at Death Row. There were no signs or indicators that Death Row was at this door.

The chaplain and I stopped and waited for a correctional officer in a booth across the hall to open the electronic gate. Once we entered, the officer closed the door behind us, and we were in a small area approximately eight feet by eight feet—another waiting area. Eight feet from the electronic door was another electronic door, and we waited in this small, closed area for the officer to open the next door. Of all my previous trips into prison, I had never seen two high-security gates so close to each other. I wondered if this were a message for the men on Death Row—that if for some reason they were able to escape one security gate, only eight feet later they would encounter another barrier.

Once through the second security gate, I was surprised by the brightly lit hallway with clean white walls. The floors were gray, and everything else was this dark red color, including the doors and window frames to rooms. The incarcerated men I saw in the hall wore red jumpsuits too. I knew the men on Death Row wore red, but I did not know that red was the color of their prison.

We went down the hall and entered through a door that led to a large, two-story common area for incarcerated men. The room, called a POD, must have been thirty to forty feet tall from floor to ceiling. Around the perimeters of the POD, a walkway separated the main court area from the cells. The walkway and the court were divided by

Plexiglas encased with a dark red window framing. Individual cells were on the other side of the walkway, and each cell door was also painted dark red. At one end of the large court, a dark red staircase led to the second floor of the common area. Even its railings were red.

I had been inside prisons many times—preaching, teaching, sharing testimonies, and singing—but the dark red on Death Row caught me by surprise. My new task was to open my eyes—to try to make sense of the situation and locate any differences between life in General Population and life on Death Row.

TWO

Joy Refreshes and Renews

Before my first visit to Death Row, I had moved from Denver, Colorado, to Durham, North Carolina. A number of painful events were the impetus for this move (I'll share more about those later), but the move did not come without pain of its own.

Leaving Denver was a tough time. I'd given up pastoring the church I had grown to love, as it was facing some of its most challenging times. Though I had pleaded with God for a chance to pastor, suddenly I was resigning from the position I wanted.

I had not been upfront with my preacher friends about my situation, and they must have wondered why I had struggled in isolation without turning to them for aid, counsel, or comfort. Leaving Denver also meant leaving Denver Children's Home and the Family-to-Family effort I had championed. There I had gained a reputation of being able to bridge the gap between governmental agencies with nongovernmental agencies. In this human-services circle, I was valued and respected. I had even gained a level of notoriety.

I had become a known person in Denver, and for good reasons. But Durham was a city where the only people who knew me were my daughter, Tiffany, and her new family. I knew this would be a transition time for my wife, Lynne, and me. I was giving up my career goals, and Lynne was giving up her job as we moved toward uncertainty. I had applied online for a position with Durham County Social Services as a child-protection caseworker, was offered the job, and moved to Durham with little more than that. The move signified the end of one season and the beginning of another.

If I were to classify my adult years in Denver, I would say they literally and figuratively ended in the cold of winter. The Colorado Holiday Blizzards occurred in the last two weeks of December 2006, paralyzing the whole Colorado Front Range. I was supposed to be in Durham by January 8, and the first blizzard on December 20 created snowdrifts up to eight feet high. Denver typically keeps moving during snowstorms, but this time, the city came to a halt. The streets were closed. The airport was closed. The stores were closed. There was no USPS, FedEx, or UPS delivery for an entire week. People were trapped in their homes during one of the busiest times of the year: Christmas.

I recall assuming the weather and roads would clear up and I could carry on with my drive after the first of the new year. Then a second blizzard hit, and I began to worry I would not make it to Durham for my new job. The weather forecasts showed *another* snowstorm due to hit Denver on January 4. The news reports on January 3 indicated that Interstate 70, east of Denver, had been reopened after being closed the better part of ten days. There was a one-day window before the next snowstorm, so I packed my car and slid out of town. Once I got fifty miles outside of Denver, the roads were cleared entirely, and I was on my way.

The blizzards of 2006 ended my time in Denver. Just as the cold weather paralyzed the city of Denver, my spirit felt the same. In many ways, I felt I'd done much good serving the church and serving families through human-service organizations. I had made a mark, having helped many individuals and even having helped restructure some organizations. Although these positives were a reality, I felt defeated and deeply stuck—just like everyone was stuck under the blizzard's control. I felt stuck as a failed pastor, a failed husband, a failed father who could not rescue his daughter. I had a brief window to get out of my personal blizzard and get to Durham.

An Introduction to Prison Ministry

Unbeknownst to me, preaching in prison began before I knew that prison preaching would play a significant role in my life. During my drive to Durham, I arranged to spend a night with my sister, Patricia, and her husband, Rick, in Little Rock, Arkansas. Rick and Patricia Shade had been doing prison ministry for years in Des Moines, Iowa. Now Patricia had a position that provided services to women at the Arkansas Department of Corrections.

When I called Patricia to ask about staying with them, she said she was going to the prison that evening for a worship service. If I was interested, she said, I could bring the sermon to the women incarcerated. I sent her my vital information and was cleared to go inside the prison gates in Arkansas.

I had been to the Denver County Jail numerous times while working for Denver Human Services, but this was my first time going into a women's prison. Immediately I was hit by the volume of noise that the women were making. There was so much chatter I had not expected. Although they were not all young women, they reminded me of teenage girls vying for attention. The noise was probably magnified because all the noise was bouncing off the cement floor, cement walls, and metal bars. No noise-reducing materials absorbed the constant words being thrown around inside the prison.

Patricia carried me to a community room where chairs were set up in a theater style. The women gathered in, at least fifty of them. They read Scripture and said prayers. Patricia led them in an old spiritual she had turned into a gospel song. "Lord, I Want to Be a Christian" was a song we sang at home and in the church we were raised in. When we were kids, my mother sang that song around the house as she did her chores. She would sing it slowly with a free-flowing tempo that caused the hearers to meditate on each word she sang:

> *Lord, I want to be a Christian*
> *In-na my heart; in-na my heart.*
> *Lord, I want to be a Christian*
> *In-na my heart.*

My sister played it with an upbeat tempo, and the women knew the song. They started singing and clapping to the beat as soon she started playing. They sang the chorus with a continuing fast-beat repetition:

> *In-na my heart; in-na my heart.*
> *In-na my heart; in-na my heart.*
> *In-na my heart; in-na my heart.*
> *In-na my heart; in-na my heart.*
> *Lord, I want to be a Christian*
> *In-na my heart.*

As the women who were locked up sang, a genuine desire to be a Christian burst out in this incarcerated congregation. I could tell they meant what they were singing that night.

My sister introduced me to them, and I stood for the first time before a group to preach in prison. My scripture text was John 14:2, which says, "In my Father's house are many mansions" (KJV). I preached about the destination of discipleship being God's house. I told them their Arkansas prison cell was not their final home, that God had better locations for them. As an example, I told them about my first bus trip from Dallas to Denver. Before I boarded the bus in Dallas, someone came over a loudspeaker to tell us the bus for Denver was about to leave. But first we'd make stops in Wichita Falls, Amarillo, Pueblo, and Colorado Springs. I told those women that they, too, were just at a stop on their way to the Father's house.

I encouraged them to have faith in Jesus Christ—and that faith would help them make it past this stop at a correctional institution. Some of the women approached me after the worship and thanked me for encouraging them. I was transitioning from Denver to Durham with my own stop at a prison in Arkansas, and I received a healthy dose of joy during my stopover with incarcerated women that night. It was not my destination, but it was a preview of the joy I would experience in years to come. Those women and the power of God within them blessed my life, and my presence blessed their lives. That is what prison ministry should look like.

A New Start in Durham

When I moved to Durham for my new job, it meant Lynne had to finish all the final packing and arrangements before leaving Denver. This was a stressful time for her, but she managed to do it and get almost all our worldly possessions into the mover's truck. In the meantime, I started my training with the North Carolina child-protection system.

In Denver, my opinions were golden. In Durham, I was informed, "We don't do things that way here." Even though I was older than the other new caseworkers, I accepted that I was still new to this system. I settled in and started investigating calls that came into the child-protection hotline. Anybody who knows anything about child-protection work knows that the volume of work surpasses what most normal human beings can do in an eight-hour day. Plus, the type of work is emotionally taxing.

At that moment I was not interested in finding a church to serve. Still, I wanted us to find a church where Lynne's musical gifts could be utilized—one where she could connect with a ministry that practiced various Christian musical genres. I wanted Lynne to be happy, and I wanted my ministry out of sight. I did not want it to be a driving factor in my life and our family. My goal was to surrender my ambitions and to see Lynne flourish. She had missed out as I held onto my cocktail of swirling ambitions.

While I was dropping off some shirts at the dry cleaner one day, a man hurried in behind me. His name was Robert Jones. He said, "Hey, I saw your Colorado license plates and wanted to talk to you. I don't see too many Black folk from Colorado." He indicated that he used to live in Boulder, and I told him I used to work in Boulder and live in Denver.

Robert and I talked for nearly an hour. We talked about Daddy Bruce's BBQ, the Denver Broncos, the Denver Nuggets, and the Colorado Rockies. We delved into national politics and how we agreed that President Bush was making many blunders, but we were excited about the possibility of Barack Obama's candidacy for president. I remember Robert telling me, "That man knows how to speak and get everybody excited."

I concurred. "I hope the media doesn't try to assassinate his message," I said, "and that nobody tries to actually assassinate him." We both basked in the potential of a Black man having a legitimate chance at becoming president of the United States.

At the end of our conversation, we talked about church and our wives. He told me his wife, Alma, was the minister of music at Mount Level Missionary Baptist Church, and I told him my wife was a church musician. I also told him my wife read music, played by ear, and had perfect pitch. He stated his wife did too. As we were leaving the dry cleaner, Robert stopped me and said, "My wife needs some help. Would you mind if she called your wife about filling in for her?" I gave him our home phone number.

Alma Jones called Lynne that evening to arrange for her to play in a rehearsal at Mount Level. A few Sundays later, Lynne played for the choirs and worship services in a fill-in role. Then weeks later, Alma and Mount Level hired Lynne to be a regular pianist. I was happy Lynne had landed in a place where her giftedness was being used and paid.

After Lynne was hired, we joined Mount Level as members. When we started attending, I did not know that the pastor of the church, Dr. William C. Turner Jr., was one of the longest-serving professors at Duke University Divinity School. I just knew I liked his preaching because he did not have "canned sermons"; he always wrestled with the Word of God and made it relevant to current culture. After we were members for a few weeks, I met with Dr. Turner, and we talked about my past ministry and service in the church. I noted that I valued his academic achievements, and I made a statement that changed the ministry trajectory in my life. I said, "I always wanted to go to seminary."

His response was short and straightforward. He said, "Apply." That night I looked up Duke Divinity School, found their application, and started working on everything required. Before long I was accepted, and I told Dr. Turner I would help at the church in whatever way I could as an associate minister.

One day in 2008, while I was a student and an associate minister, another associate minister named Joe Hall asked me to come to Durham's Guess Road Prison to preach. He headed up the church's prison ministry, and when I accepted his invitation, my connection to prison ministry took a substantial turn. For three years, I preached regularly at Guess Road until the state closed the facility in 2011. The closing of this prison left a void in my ministry because I had been preaching there at least once a month and often twice a month.

In 2011 I also graduated from Duke. During this season in my life, I had the wisdom to allow God to lead me in my pursuits. I did not to try to dictate the direction I wanted God to take me. I had to reimagine how God worked within a minister so God's message could be revealed to God's people. The opportunities to preach on Death Row, as well as other types of ministry opportunities that would later be extended to me, were rare and in some ways unique. Many preachers would cherish the chance to preach on Death Row because this population is often the most notorious of all those incarcerated. Many would love to do it and seek opportunities to do so, but as I will explain, I was *invited* to preach there. As I would soon learn, I would have to imagine ministry differently than I had in the past. I had yet to fully discover how each trip to Death Row would give me new avenues to explore how joy can refresh and renew.

THREE

Unexpected Joy

From October 2016 through December 15, 2017, I made thirty-three trips to Unit 3 at Central Prison in Raleigh, North Carolina. Unit 3 is the formal name for Death Row at Central Prison. Before ever going to minister on Death Row, I concluded that the death penalty was a fallacious practice that did not serve the community, the victims, or those sentenced with good outcomes. During these fourteen months of my life, my views were confirmed about capital punishment in Western cultures being a misguided notion and the most inappropriate response to criminal behavior.

I joined the group of volunteers in a POD, where no residents lived. I was surprised because the POD was spotlessly clean and well lit. I had been in PODs in several prisons, and none were this clean. I suspected it was clean because it was not lived in and was used as a room for large group activities. One Death Row resident in the room was busy moving tables and supplies around for our arrival. This man, dressed in a red jumpsuit, was fulfilling some duties he had been assigned to prepare for our ministry. We volunteers were there as part of Short Journey, a ministry that specialized in three-day events for men on Death Row.

The Death Row resident was full of smiles and courtesy to the volunteers coming into the POD. He engaged in a conversation with the correctional officer supervising us in the POD. Soon, the correctional officer and the man who was incarcerated were laughing as if they were coworkers who had learned some detail that only coworkers could enjoy. I did not know what they were laughing about, but I did sense that they did not see each other as enemies at that moment.

If I had any notions of men on Death Row as tortured individuals living bitter lives, scowling and hissing their way through each day, this resident replaced them. This man stood about thirty feet from me, working, smiling, and laughing with a correctional officer. At this point, I did not yet know I would be preaching about joy on Death Row, but my first experience there was seeing a man serving his time on Death Row with some measure of joy in his life.

Soon the Short Journey volunteers gathered for a brief meeting to discuss our agenda for the day. We formed a circle to pray for the speakers and the men we had never met. As we placed our arms around one another's shoulders, we prayed that the men coming to Short Journey would have a blessed experience. After our prayer, the volunteers were assigned to specific tables. At each of four tables, three volunteers would host six Death Row residents. After we set out name tags, folders, pens, and paper supplies, the three of us at our table huddled up like a small football team, placing our arms around one another once again. We then prayed specifically for one another and for the men who would be coming to our table.

The residents soon showed up outside the entrance to the POD. The Plexiglas separating the POD from the outside hallway allowed us all to see one another. The residents outside looking in seemed curious but hesitant about what they were about to experience. They had not been told much about what to expect—only that it would be a three-day event with Christian men who were bringing the gospel. They also knew the food served would not be their regular prison food.

As the residents looked in on us, we looked out at them as volunteers. We were encouraged to be welcoming—to present as excited about the opportunity to share our time with these men. One obvious demographic was easy to notice: that I was the only person of color among the Short Journey volunteers. In other experiences with prison ministry where I was the only Black person, I have witnessed Black incarcerated residents saying, "What do all these White men want?" or "What are these White men up to?"

As the men filtered into the POD, our roles reversed somewhat. The men on Death Row presented as even more excited than the volunteers who were told to show excitement about the upcoming days. For the most part, the men entered with smiles and warm handshakes. There was almost a giddy joyfulness coming from these men who had the sentence of death covering their lives. I was strangely encouraged. Any of my anxious thoughts or reservations about what to expect from these men were swept away by these men's enthusiastic arrival for the first day's activities.

My prior understanding of Death Row came from what I had seen in the movies. These images proved to be completely different from what I was to experience on Death Row at Central Prison. *The Green Mile*'s gloomy depiction of John Coffey did not align with my experience. The physical barriers established between Sister Helen Prejean and Death Row resident Matthew Poncelet in the movie version of *Dead Man Walking* did not exist. On the contrary, Death Row was clean and bright to the eye, and the men were able to walk up to me, reach out their hands for a shake or a fist bump, and say hello with smiles on their faces. I felt like giving them each a hug, but hugs are not tolerated at Central Prison. All contact between those incarcerated and volunteers must be limited to a handshake or a fist bump.

All the men's jumpsuits were the same shade of red, with the exception of those that had evidently been washed many times. Whether the red jumpsuits were newer or older, it did not make a difference to the men.

The men selected to participate in this three-day Short Journey experience were sent to their assigned tables. There, they would have conversations about predetermined topics with one another and with the volunteers. One of the volunteers at each table was a designated clergy volunteer responsible for keeping the spiritual focus of the table discussion on target. They could also aid anyone at the table who might need prayer or have questions they didn't want to bring up during table discussion time.

While at the "family table" to which I had been assigned, I quickly became familiar with the men. Of the six residents at our table, one identified as a Muslim. Later, while doing my Clinical Pastoral Education (CPE), I learned that those incarcerated in North Carolina must designate their religious preferences—or lack thereof—when they begin their incarceration. For the most part, the incarcerated were not allowed to attend or participate in activities sponsored by other religions. So the Christians were only allowed to participate in Christian services, and Muslims were only allowed to participate in Muslim services. Short Journey and Kairos, which I had previously worked with, were both Christian organizations, but in *some* situations, men of other religions were allowed to attend the three- and four-day activities.

The Muslim gentleman was seated immediately to my left. Later, I found out that seating happened intentionally because they wanted a clergyperson to address any scriptural or theological dilemmas that might arise between Christian and Muslim understandings and practices. This individual was completely respectful of Christian concepts. At the same time, he was confident about his own beliefs and did not attempt to insist his religion was better than Christianity. When he saw differences, he simply pointed out how Muslims practiced their faith.

I intentionally sought to return respect to this man, and I believe I gave him some new insights about Christianity. We were both in our sixties and both Black, and our stories paralleled each other more than the differences in our religion. Despite our different faith walks, a joy surfaced between the two of us because we both sought to respect each other. When I would see him in later visits to Death Row, the two of us would take a moment to see how the other was doing.

Joy raised its banner during those three days. The men sentenced to death surprised me repeatedly with their desire to be alive and their commitment to living their best lives in a place designed to rob them of joy. They brought sobriety mixed with pleasure, and they understood the gravity of their situation and gave the grimness of their situation honest reflections. Still, they also brought a desire to hold and express freedom of heart and mind. Their longing for freedom showed in their smiles, laughter, jokes, and playfulness with one another, the prison staff, and even the volunteers. Each day I tried to carry joy with me to the men on Death Row, but I discovered the men on Death Row adding joy into *my* life.

I had the responsibility to talk with them about forgiveness. I ended my talk by telling them that forgiveness means getting another chance. I revised and shared an old Billy Graham illustration to press my point.[1] My version of the illustration went like this:

> A middle school group was visiting a museum and came across a painting titled *Checkmate*. The picture depicted an old scheming chess player placing a young man in the final game status of checkmate. In the painting, the young man was dejected, and the older man laughed as he triumphed over the younger man. One of the boys in the class was an avid chess player, and as his class moved on to the next location, he lingered at the painting.
>
> Suddenly the student started yelling in the quietness of the museum, "It's a lie! It's a lie! It's a lie!" The student's teacher came rushing back to him to see what was wrong. Then the boy told her the picture was a lie. "He has one more move!" he said.

I informed the men on Death Row that someone had pronounced checkmate on their lives, but their lives were not over. Every day they woke up, they had one more move. I lifted my index finger to the air and said, "Today, I have one more move." If they saw one another in the days to come and noticed one of them was down, I challenged them to lift an index finger and remind their buddy of his "one more move." Following that day, every time I came back, a few of the men would just walk by me and lift their index fingers to let me know that both they and I had at least one more move.

On this trip, my first time on Death Row at Central Prison, my life was forever changed. During a break for snacks was when the man immediately to my right turned to me and declared, "I have decided that I am not on 'Death Row.' I am on 'Life Row,' and I am going to live my life every day the best way I can." This statement expressed a core understanding that I was gaining regarding how joy works in our lives. I have discovered that joy is best experienced when you pursue it, even if you are in the middle of what might be considered horrible conditions.

When writing about Death Row, it is tempting to write about all the evils of the criminal justice system in the United States of America and how the death penalty is the ultimate example of these injustices. I believe the criminal justice system is corrupt at the core and that our entire approach to criminal justice needs reform from a retributive justice, to a restorative justice, and eventually to a liberation justice system. I also believe the death penalty needs to be outlawed as the highest and cruelest form of injustice. Racism and slavery were at the genesis of the flawed criminal justice system that we all are victimized by today. Much has been written about this, and since the system still exists, much still needs to be written and discussed. This book, however, is not about that. This effort shows how joy has worked in the lives of men and women who have found themselves under the curse of this corrupt system. As I write, I hope to show how joy is powerful enough to reach into the lives of those who have been told their lives need to be destroyed.

Preaching Joy on Death Row

My journey to Death Row began a choice to pursue joy. At the end of 2015, I made an unusual decision for myself. I decided to seek a path of discovery—my quest for the upcoming year. As such, I decided to pursue joy in the year 2016. I wanted to learn about joy and how to experience joy in my own life. I wanted the theory comprehension regarding joy, but more than that, I wanted my year to be flooded with joyful experiences. For whatever increase in understanding of joy I gained, I wanted that knowledge to enhance my personal experiences with joy.

At every turn, I intentionally sought to include joy in all events at home or work or in ministry activity. Time with my family, neighbors, the clients I served, or parishioners at church needed to recognize joy or be injected with it. When I was involved in planning work or church events, I sought to add joy as a topic of discussion. I made joy the thread that tied my routines together.

In that October Short Journey, the senior chaplain, Teresa Stratton, was present during my talk. Afterward, she asked if I was available to join her team of preachers who volunteer to preach on Sundays to both the men on Death Row and the men in General Population. I agreed to help. She also asked if I could preach the Christmas message in December 2016 to the men on Death Row. I agreed to that also.

I was convinced that my pursuit of joy was something I needed to share with the men on Death Row. In past years, I'd had many prison experiences with men and a few with women, and amid my time with these believers, I'd found some of the most genuine expressions of worship. The questions that swirled in my mind included: *How is the message of joy interpreted by the group of men who have been sentenced to die at the hand of the State of North Carolina? Is there a special interpretation of Scripture related to Death Row worshipers? And how do Death Row worshipers relate to Scripture?* I began to explore joy for a new perspective, where those who might be considered "the least of these" could share what joy is all about.

From December 2016 to June 2017, I preached five times to the men on Death Row. One was the sermon about Christmas joy. The other four sermons were delivered during weekly Sunday worship services on Death Row. The attendance varied from twenty-two to twenty-seven at each gathering, but ultimately, I was able to reach about seventy-five residents.

I made special effort to prepare and present an empowering message to the men. I wanted them to get the best I had. I preached and served as if I were going to a palace to bring a message to all the dignitaries of the land. Though others may be more gifted at both sermon writing and sermon delivery, I gave those on Death Row quality workmanship. I think that is the optimal way to minister to those incarcerated. Some who serve the incarcerated offer half-baked efforts, believing those who are locked up should be grateful for whatever they get. Behind the prison doors, however, I had the opportunity to see Jesus Christ in the very way He said, "I was in prison, and you visited me" (Matthew 25:36 NLT). I gave to the incarcerated as if I were giving to my Lord. I did my best, believing my efforts would be rewarded.

From August to December 2017, I completed a unit of CPE with the University of North Carolina Hospitals that required ten hours per week of service in the community. To meet my requirement, I was allowed to return to Death Row weekly to sit with small groups of men (two to four). In these meetings, I shared brief statements from the five sermons they had already heard and asked them to write out their responses to the statements. I asked them to first write whether they agreed with the statements and why, then I asked them to tell me stories from their lives that demonstrated how the words were true or false. This search for a practical validation of joy and the gospel of Jesus Christ was the most rewarding ministerial experience in my life. These men opened up and poured out their testimonies of renewal, describing how their faith had led to their personal and communal joy.

During my weekly visits for my CPE, I asked if it were possible to engage the women on Death Row with these sermons and get their responses too. Then arrangements were made for me to share a message with the three women on North Carolina's Death Row. At the first meeting, I played a video of the sermon I submitted to the Yale Center for Faith & Culture and got responses from the women. In the second meeting, we read my joy sermon about Naomi and Ruth. I immediately got responses from the women regarding that message.

My meetings with the women on Death Row were filled with both laughter and solemnity. During every visit, I tried to give them the same respect I give the women who make up the leadership efforts at every church I have attended. As you journey with me through this book, I will mention my experiences and the writings of the men and women on Death Row, though I regret that none of the women's writing will be shared here because I do not have their permission. I wish I could share the women's words with you, but unfortunately, I can only share the men's stories.

When I first asked the men to write their responses, I worried about exposing their identities if I shared what they wrote. The system often misuses those who are incarcerated, and many people make money off the incarcerated person's plight. I did not want to take advantage of their circumstance if I found a way to publish their writings. As such, my plan was to use only their initials. But early in the process, a group of the men asked me about using their names. They *wanted* their names attached to their writings. They thought that using their initials robbed them of their identities. I gathered that they were tired of being hidden in a system that does not value them. Later, after I received all the responses, I adopted the process of signed release forms. Subsequently, I went back and acquired waivers from almost every man.

Throughout this book, I'll share the handwritten responses from these men, along with their names to respect their wishes. I chose to include their responses as they wrote them by hand because I believe the images offer a window into who they are. If you have any difficulty reading their handwriting, transcripts are available online. For more information, see the resources section at the back of the book. Inmates' handwritten responses have been preserved in their original writing style when referenced outside of the letter provided.

FOUR

Joy Is God's Work

U nlike during the sermon series, these small group sessions gave me the opportunity to sit face-to-face with the men, talk, and listen to their stories and feelings. I was delighted when most of the thirty or so who had attended worship showed up at one time or another for the sessions. We met in the community room, a thirty-by-thirty well-lit concrete block of a space with a high ceiling. One wall had two thick metal doors in each corner with an oversize window in between. It was a barren place, and a correctional officer was always present, sitting or standing nearby.

After they considered the first sermon I delivered at Christmas in 2016, I asked the men their thoughts on the core difference between the Christian perspective of joy and other disciplines. Many people believe joy is a pursuit, something gained by human endeavor, or that joy is the conclusion of a good decision, a fortunate turn of luck, or even a shopping spree.

We discussed when the shepherds were confronted by an angel in the book of Luke. The shepherds were poor and typically despised in Palestine in the days of Christ's birth. Like many people in modern society, they were trying to survive in a system where finances determined their status. In the story, an angel was dispatched from heaven to tell this ill-considered group that God was working to bring them joy.

I asked the men on Death Row to consider how they might compare themselves to the shepherds as poor men trying to stay alive in a system dependent on money. It is safe to say no one on Death Row in North Carolina is financially secure. None afforded an attorney to defend themselves in their capital cases—cases in which legal costs are high.

Christianity is distinct from most other major religions because it is not built on good behavior leading to good outcomes. Christianity is about getting to know God regardless of what you have done or what has happened to you. It is about experiencing God rather than using God to get what you want. The struggle for those who call themselves Christian is not between doing good or doing bad; it is between trying to get it right and enjoying God.

When our vision of joy is a product of human personal construction, we take God out of the joy factor. God is the chief architect that designs our joy. God is the general contractor overseeing our joy. God is the financer with all the resources required for our joy. God makes joy the mortar that holds our structures sturdy. Without God, there is no joy, whether we realize it or not. God can even take the awfulness of capital punishment to construct a cathedral of joy in the hearts of those facing the death penalty.

A joy that relies on human accomplishment is selfish. It points us away from God. Saint Augustine, a fourth-century theologian and philosopher, wrestled with pursuits of self-gratification hundreds of years ago. In his famed *Confessions*, he wrote, "My sin consisted in this, that I sought pleasure, sublimity, and truth not in God but in his creatures, in myself and other created beings."[2] Augustine revealed that nothing in life can match turning to the Creator as the source of joy.

The men and women on Death Row have seen the negative side of life, especially in the criminal justice system. In addition to having to face the monetary strength of the State against them in their criminal cases, they are despised and condemned by a State that has determined their lives to be worthless.

Knowing they are considered throwaway people, I pressed the residents of Death Row to wrestle with these three questions concerning my sermon:

- Do you feel God is working to bring joy into your life?
- How does God fit into explaining where you are and what you have to live with and without on Death Row?
- Is joy available when you face your crimes or charges or sentences or separation from family and society?

As you will see in their writings, the men were clear about God's joy in their lives even within a maximum-security prison.

Writing prompt for those who are incarcerated:

The term *joy* in its dictionary definition means the emotion of great delight or happiness caused by something exceptionally good or satisfying. That means, something happens, and the thing that happens makes you feel good. Christian joy has another definition. Christian joy is an assurance that God uses circumstances to bring believers good feelings that rest not on events but on God's work in their lives. The difference is that Christian joy understands that God is intentionally working to bring us joy as opposed to joy being dependent on happenstance.

Did I Commit an Unforgivable Sin?

John McNeill, who went by "Mac," often brought a wide smile and a serious disposition to our worship services. He was a joyous worshiper and thoughtful when he shared from his heart.

In February 1993, Mac was indicted for first-degree burglary and first-degree murder of a woman he'd been dating. After being tried capitally, the jury returned a guilty verdict for first-degree burglary as well as for first-degree murder "on the theories of premeditation and deliberation and felony murder." On the basis of his murder conviction, the jury recommended he receive the death penalty.[3]

Mac made a powerful statement of how he has changed his way of thinking as a Christian. He wrote, "I committ a sin that would never be forgiving for (murder), but I read the Holy Bible and the word of God said He would forgive all sin but one. Did I committ the unforgive sin" (see fig. 4.1). Until he read the Bible for himself, Mac understood murder to be what the Bible refers to as the single unforgivable sin. He thought God would not or could not forgive him. The idea that God forgives all sins blossomed into true joy for Mac.

Mac's other comment hit me hard. Today, he is not where he wants to be, but he still finds joy. I was not where I wanted to be when I met Mac. During the time in my life when I first met these men, I wanted desperately to pastor a local congregation. I had been a candidate for numerous pastoral positions, none of which had worked out. Though I am prone to self-pity and regret, Mac taught me that I can have joy even when I don't have the things I want in life.

I find joy Knowing what God is doing for me in my circumstance. Though, I not were I want to be, but it is a delight to Know God's will never leave me and it bring me joy ever day of my life. Because we have a Savior who will never forsake me (us) - When I want to give up He tell me He love me unconclition and die on the cross for us all. The joy He give can not be measure nor explain by the World joy.

STORY

I committ a sin that would never be forgiving for (murder), but I read the Holy Bible and The word of God said He would forgive all sin but one. Died, I committ the unforgive sin. Reading the book and I read God's Holy word I could not put it down cause once you taste God's word it is sweeter than Honey comb. That is when I found out that I was forgave of all my sin. I been reading God's word every since and aply it to my life and tell other of His Goodness. Thank You Jesus for the joy You brought to me, the devil mention Evil for me, but You are truly the Joy of my life.

Figure 4.1. Response from John "Mac" McNeill

I Never Want to Move About Without Christ Jesus

I'll not soon forget the first Sunday I preached on Death Row—one reason being Melvin White Jr., who approached me after the sermon and asked if he could have my words to share with his family. There are strict rules against volunteers and the incarcerated exchanging any items, so the on-duty correctional officer who attended the worship service had to approve it. The officer said he would make a copy, then three other people who were incarcerated asked for copies as well.

Melvin had been indicted in July 1995 for two counts of first-degree murder and then in September 1995 for first-degree burglary. He was tried and found guilty of capital offenses. The jury recommended the death sentence for the first-degree murder cases, and he was sentenced to 82–108 months for his burglary conviction.[4] On numerous occasions Melvin has indicated that he is not guilty and should not be on Death Row.

The week before I met with Melvin in the small group, he was afforded a trip to a hospital for testing. Outside the prison walls, Melvin saw all the things that he could not touch and enjoy. Can you imagine how looking at the trees, seeing restaurants open, or watching people throw a frisbee or walk their dogs in a park would haunt you if you knew you would never experience freedom again? He was angry with himself for being incarcerated.

Melvin's anger fizzled, though, once he had the chance to reflect on how God's love provided him salvation—and that salvation was his ultimate reward. On my own journey, things that I could not experience have also caused me internal angst. Melvin helped me realize there will always be things beyond my reach. There will always

My joy is in Christ Jesus is due to What He has done and is still doing in my life. I'm not saying that I walk around each day laughing as if I'm a lunatic, and yes I have moments of difficulties. I want to be free, to be with my family, to go as I once was able to. But I never want to move about without Christ Jesus, everywhere I go I want HIM to already prepared my way. My joy is in Christ and the peace I have in my life is due to HIM and the guidance that HE gives me daily. No one Nothing can save my soul, give me peace, answer my prayers even though it can be (yes, no, or wait).

<u>Story</u>
— One of my most difficult moments was last Friday Sept/22/2017. I had to go to the outside hospital, and while riding I observed the trees, fresh air, nature. I saw how much I was missing or how much I thought I was/am missing in life, and I got upset. But when I stop to think all that God is and has worked in my life, how I once was lost, headed to hell, I haven't repented yet, but I will, as soon as I get back to the pod, to my assigned cell.

God is so good to me, because he could have left me where I was, in my life's mess, but HE had compassion, mercy on me, He called me to His side as a father, his son. Now I know I'm saved and peace has filled my life, this is what I understand about my trip the the hospital, God is/did show me that HE's still in control and I'm not missing anything.

Figure 4.2. Response from Melvin White Jr.

be higher heights, and there will always be inadequacies. But, like Melvin, it's crucial for me and you to embrace the greater spiritual rewards that God provides now and in salvation.

In his response (see fig. 4.2), you'll see how after his short break from isolation, Melvin was able to realize, "I want to be free . . . but I never want to move about without Christ Jesus."

Months after that first sermon, Melvin said he mailed a copy of my words to his family, and they found value in the words too. This brought me joy.

I Wish I Had What You Got

Alden Harden is beloved on Death Row and is a constant Christian advocate who encourages others. He serves regularly in worship and helps lead the liturgy.

In October 1993 Alden was indicted for the first-degree murder of two police officers, who were shot as they attempted arrest. The jury found him guilty on both charges of murder "on the theory of premeditation and deliberation." The jury recommended death, and the trial court followed their recommendation.[5]

Alden shared how a fellow man who was incarcerated once said to him, "I wish I had what you got" (see fig. 4.3). He assigned no part of achieving joy to his abilities or diligence, nor to the work or efforts of others. To Alden, joy was about allowing Jesus into his heart. His joy was raised counter to the negative pulls against the human spirit that occur on Death Row.

I have never spoken those words aloud to anyone, but in the secret of my heart, I have wished that other people's privileges were mine. As a child, I wanted the new toys or bicycles other kids had. As a young preacher, I wanted the advantages from which other young ministers benefited: academic benefits, status, and even giftedness in the pulpit. As I started my service journey on Death Row, I was in a funk. I wanted the experiences other pastors were having. Alden showed me that wanting what others had was never going to satisfy my soul's craving. None of us will achieve real joy if we are constantly absorbed in what we don't have. These days, as I recount my blessings,

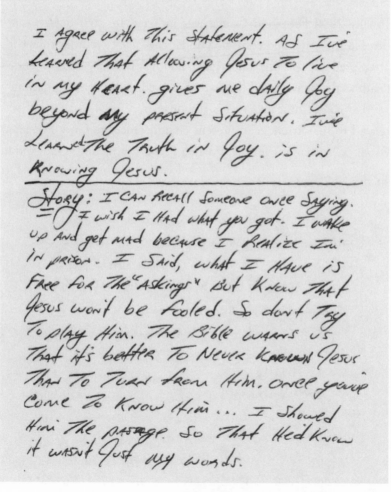

Figure 4.3. Response from Alden Harden

several people have told me they wish they had what I have: an abundance of joy. My response is that everyone can have it. It's free for the taking to those who open themselves to God.

Just Like Jonah

In July 2000 Fernando Garcia was indicted for first-degree murder. He was tried and convicted under the "felony murder rule, with attempted rape as the underlying felony." The jury recommended death as the penalty, and the court followed that recommendation.[6]

Fernando indicated in his response (see fig. 4.4) that joy was related to his surrender of present circumstances to God. Fernando wrote, "Christian joy for me is: when I give a thing unto God, and in

Christian Joy for me is:- When I give a Thing unto God, and in my faith with patience I Know in my heart God will see this "Thing" through. The Joy comes from intimately knowing God. Joy comes from me Knowing that All Things passes through God's hands. There is Nothing that God does not Know About, or Cannot handle, and though in my limited Nature and feebleness I have trouble doing things on my own. Joy comes from Knowing God is with me!! God the Creator "See All" and "Knows All." and since God created All, Since He sits on the throne, He Knows how to get me out of, or deliver me from All trouble.

My Joy comes from Knowing that:
"God's faithfulness is my protecting shield."

STORY:

God uses everything, or creates circumstances and, situations for his glory.
It's like me coming to prison here, in NC, instead
of NJ. I have no doubt God brought me to
NC prison to save my life. Also in here it
is not as bad as a NJ prison where I might
have to constantly be looking-out for someone
who might want to take my life. But in here

it is not so. So then, here I can be more focused
on seeking God. Have my character built.
Just like "Jonah", when he entered the
Big fish's belly. God is working on me. I
have seen it in my attitude, my softness of
heart for others. Believe me when I tell
you that if I hear a sad story, I tear-up
Bigtime?? And in the process of building me
up God has touched my heart to feel good, and
joyous because I can feel God's hand on me.
I would have never thought about tithing and
now I can't wait til I receive money to send
in my tithes. Because I can receive a "CD"
series that I send to people. I worry about
others not hearing God's word. My joy comes
from giving out God's word.

Figure 4.4. Response from Fernando Garcia

41

my faith with patience I know in my heart God will see this 'thing' through. The joy comes from intimately knowing God. Joy comes from me knowing that *all* things passes through God's hands." To Fernando, joy was what God would provide, but he (Fernando) needed to turn it over to God and stop trying to oversee things on his own. He compared himself to Jonah, who waited for God to do God's good work after being swallowed by the big fish. He also told the story of how joy made him think of others since being on Death Row. He continued: "I would have never thought about tithing and now I can't wait til I receive money to send in my tithes. Because I can receive a 'CD' series that I send to people. I worry about others not hearing God's word. My joy comes from giving out God's Word." Fernando indicated that he felt joy when he could extend the blessings of God's Word to other people.

All Things Work Together for Good

Richard Warner was found guilty of robbery with a dangerous weapon and first-degree murder.[7] A jury recommended a sentence of death, and the trial court entered judgment in accordance with that recommendation. The trial court also sentenced him to up to ten years in prison for the robbery conviction.

Another man who was incarcerated on Death Row once attacked Richard with a prison knife. Richard stated, "I defended myself . . . I could have taken his knife away and then turned it on him . . . instead . . . the Holy Spirit intervened and I used this opportunity to say to the guy that God loves him." Richard could have been injured or killed, but God brought a peaceful outcome by working through him. God's name and presence made a difference.

Richard's story reminds us that God's presence alone is enough to transform a dismal moment into a joyous moment. God can transform a bleak setting into a joy-filled atmosphere. This must be what King David meant when he said, "In your presence there is fullness of joy" (Psalm 16:11). Both King David and Richard inform us that God's nearness brings joy.

God's Grace Is Sufficient

Frank Chambers was a regular in the Sunday worship experiences on Death Row. The distinctive gray beard under his chin was eye-catching, but it was less attention-grabbing than his distinctive slow pace. When Frank entered a room, you knew he was there. There was something about his slow, intentional movements and speech that made you see him. Frank expressed to me his thoughts, and I gleaned from him that no matter how let down he may feel at times, it still gives him joy to go out into Death Row's community and visit with peers that no one else wants to be around.

Frank was tried jointly with two other men for first-degree murder, two counts of first-degree robbery with a dangerous weapon, and one count of first-degree burglary. Frank and one of the other defendants were each handed two death sentences, while the other defendant was given two life sentences.[8] During our meetings, Frank was a one-of-a-kind personality, and he seemed to utilize his distinctiveness to put himself on equal footing with those around him. Frank told me that there are times when one person does not measure up to a moment. Frank let me know that in those moments, God's grace is sufficient for us; God's grace was established before the foundation of the world began. This truth Frank held gave him joy.

Frank's joy had eternal roots that had little to do with the happenings of the current moment. While Frank did not present as an educated thinker, his thoughts probed deep into my soul. Frank made me think beyond the shallow waters of the moment to the deep waters that hold eternity. He helped me remember that God holds both my history and my future.

Look What They Did to Me

Back when I had just moved to Durham and had begun my work as a child-protection investigator, I was unknown by all the officials and staff at Durham County. I had joined Mount Level Missionary Baptist Church, where I had met Dr. William C. Turner Jr., and Lynne had been hired onto the staff at Mount Level. The job had filled a void in her life, but I continued to bury my desire to pastor.

Mount Level required an orientation class for all new members, and Lynne and I participated in this class during the Sunday school hour every week. One of the weeks included a visit with Pastor Turner. At our meeting, Pastor Turner addressed questions that caused my understanding of joy to shift. We discussed the fruit of the Spirit presented in Galatians 5:22–23: "love, joy, peace, patience, kindness, generosity, faithfulness, gentleness, and self-control." Pastor Turner explained that all these aspects of the Spirit of God are generated *by* God. As I sat there, presenting to be an upbeat minister, I asked a question he might have assumed was a general theological or biblical question but which was one I asked in seeking an answer for my struggle: "What if someone does not want to reflect the fruit of the Spirit? For instance, what if someone is sour and bitter and does not feel joy in their life?"

Pastor Turner replied that the fruit of the Spirit is not a smorgasbord or a buffet by which we pick and choose items we want. We do not get to say what and how the fruit is revealed. It is God's doing. His words gave me great pause as I sat in self-pity, mourning my belated ministerial life. I suddenly felt a prodding: God oversees joy. At that moment I came to see that joy was God's work and God's business.

I had no idea how God was going to open me to the significance of joy or how this revelation of how God oversees joy would populate and repopulate in my daily life. I did know that my mood had to change. I left that orientation class saying to myself that if God wanted me to experience joy, I had to yield myself to learning more about how God imagines joy working in my Christian walk. Shortly after this, Joe Hall engaged me to preach at Guess Road Prison.

My struggles often come from my failure to see God as the one providing joy in my life. When I sought to be the light for joy, I missed God's light and power. I often was overwhelmed with the burden of providing what only God can truly provide. In a real way, my personal pushing for joy from within was a form of idolatry. I tried to take God's place. Instead, I needed to learn that joy is God's work.

FIVE

Seeing Joy Clearly

My family struggled financially when I was young. My parents were not formally educated people, but they were hardworking and provided for the family from their labor. As a child, I did not know about being rich or poor, but as I got older and saw what money could buy, I discovered my financial status. I must have been between six and seven when a boy who lived across the street got a new bicycle to replace his old bike. I had never had a bike, and I asked my parents if I could get one. They let me know they did not have the money for it. It dawned on me that my family was not wealthy.

As I grew into adolescence, my parents' lack of formal education and financial capacity became a driving force in my life. Unlike my parents, I wanted to be formally educated, but I did not know how that would happen. I also wanted wealth, but I had no history of securing or maintaining it. I had already begun to associate wealth with being happy, or at least I figured it was a significant contributor to happiness.

We lived in Mason City, Iowa, until I was four, then in Des Moines until I was twelve years old. Then we moved to Denver,

Colorado, where I lived until I was eighteen. Many of my Des Moines memories are murky because I was visually challenged, but I did not get glasses until I was ten years old. I thought my vision was how everyone else saw. As I sat in the rear of a classroom and a teacher noticed me struggling to see what was on the chalkboard, she told me to come sit in the front of the class. She sent me home with a note telling my parents I needed glasses.

So much of my childhood desire for joy was wrapped up in wanting to have what the other kids had and to fit in with them as an equal peer. I did not want to be the odd kid or the outsider looking in. In essence, I wanted to be cool and popular. My learned reality was that I could not even see things the way other kids were seeing things. I also thought I was as intelligent and bright as any of the other kids, but when a child cannot see, it is hard to learn on the same level. Just as my vision was unclear, I probably had a vague understanding of what joy was all about.

I remember my first optometrist appointment. The optician sat in his consulting room, smoking a cigarette. He asked me some questions, told me to put my face up to this weird-looking device, and adjusted the machine to fit my then preadolescent facial frame. I looked through some fuzzy lenses, and in between cigarette puffs, he asked me to read the letters on the wall. He kept adjusting the lenses until I had clear vision in one eye. Then he repeated the same process on my other eye. Finally, at the age of ten, I could see clearly! He ordered me glasses, and in a couple of weeks, they arrived. I have worn glasses daily ever since.

In retrospect, I know my formative years were spent in a visual haze. I learned to live with general and approximate answers or solutions because I could not see specifics enough to make specific conclusions. I think my practice of accepting the broad and general approach to issues hampered my learning even after I got glasses. I was a slow learner because I was a slow reader, and from the first day I received my glasses, I realized I was substantially years behind my peers in school. I had missed so much sequential learning between kindergarten and fifth grade. I was working from an academic deficit and did not know how to get caught up.

My memories of Des Moines are somewhat dark and dreary, with long winters and blistering-hot summers. We lived in a neighborhood of older framed structures, the roads were older, the church my father pastored was in an old building converted into a church,

Dewey Williams at age ten, before he had glasses, standing with his sister Genevieve and younger nephews Timothy and Barry in Des Moines, Iowa.

and the corner store where we shopped was old too. When it snowed, the weather would remain dismal for months. Though the city was already older and gloomy, my poor eyesight further blurred the landscape. What a combination of diminished perception I lived in.

Perhaps my perception of Des Moines was captured in an event that occurred one day. When school let out, I had to walk home in the middle of an Iowa blizzard. As a kid, the walk to and from school seemed miles long, but when I went back as an adult, the walk was only about a half mile. But still, a half mile in a blizzard was a long way. When I finally got home, three bolts on the metal awning that covered the front porch had been dislodged by the strong winds. The one remaining bolt was still attached, and the awning was flipping back and forth in front of the door that would allow me entrance into my home. It indeed was one of the scariest moments of my life because I believed the awning could have killed me if it hit me. I made it in, but I was scared to my core.

Then in October 1967, when I was twelve years old, my family moved to Denver. As we pulled into town late that night, it had begun to snow hard. I remember going into our duplex—a new brick structure with new appliances, kitchen cabinets, and carpeting. I thought that duplex apartment would be the best place in the world to live.

Denver's snowflakes that night seemed to be bigger and fluffier than the snowflakes in Des Moines, but the following day when I got up, the sun was shining brightly. Within a few hours, all the streets that had been covered with snow the night before were cleared by the rays from the sun. Glasses made my vision clear in a new city. Compared to Des Moines, Denver appeared clean and fresh. I remember thinking that I lived in an old place one day and the next day I lived in a new place. Moving to Denver felt like dying and going to heaven.

I never had conversations with my parents about why they decided to leave Des Moines. I suspect they saw Denver as a new opportunity to do new things with new people. Perhaps Des Moines had become blurry to them too. Later I was told that my mother had some health problems and medical procedures in Des Moines that hampered her and put a drain on the family's finances. I suppose Denver promised a fresh and new place, which is what my parents needed. I suspect they were pursuing joy for themselves and our family.

I am the seventh of eight children, but when we moved in 1967, only three of us were still at home. The move provided a chance for my parents to start over with only three children to care for and some health problems in the rearview mirror. Providing for only three children must have seemed so much more manageable. Genevieve was three years older than me, and Patricia was two years younger. We were a new family in a new city, prepared to do things for God.

Our home in Denver was full of happiness. My father worked, my mother kept the house and did some professional babysitting, and my sisters and I went to school. We all worked and served in the new church my father started soon after moving to Denver. There was excitement. There was family joy.

In Denver, I enjoyed life as a teenager. I was not a popular kid. I was more of a loner, but I desperately wanted to be popular in my heart of hearts and wanted the girls to think I was attractive and cool. My challenge was that I did not know how to approach girls. I always felt socially unfit for the moment around them, and I was constantly holding back in public settings. Our home was exceptionally religious, so my prominent outlet to the world, other than school, was church-related activities. I sang in the high school choir and made it to a particular group that sang show tunes at special events at school and around the city. By then I had acknowledged my call to preach in church and always thought God gave me messages to share. So I started preaching when I was sixteen years old, under the tutelage of my father.

I was confident to declare that I was a preacher with great ideas, but I was as timid as a mouse around girls. As a teen, I was often told that I was a good-looking guy, but my lack of charisma and know-how made me a romantic misfit. Not knowing when to say things or what to do with girls frustrated me, which led me to cower when near them.

When I was fourteen, a girl started attending our church, and she gave me her phone number and told me to call her that night. It was the most awkward phone call of my life. We said our cordial greetings, but then there was utter silence. I didn't know what to say. After a couple of minutes, the girl said, "If you don't have anything to talk about, I got to go." We said goodbye to each other, marking the end of our relationship.

At age fifteen, I met a girl at a state Baptist youth meeting who invited me to go to a drive-in movie with her, her older sister, and her older sister's boyfriend. The sister and her boyfriend were in the car's front seat, and the girl who invited me and I were in the back seat. During the movie, the sister and her boyfriend disappeared below the front car seat—doing something other than watching the movie. After a few minutes, the sister lifted her head, looked back at us, and said, "Y'all ain't doing nothin' back there?" The truth was, I had never kissed a girl before, let alone done anything that would mean disappearing below a car seat.

When I was seventeen, I had a girlfriend. She was beautiful, and many guys wanted to date her, but I was the lucky one. After a few weeks of holding hands and kissing following church events, she invited me to her house one afternoon, indicating that a few kids were going to be over. I arrived, and six other teenagers were sitting around her living room just having fun. I sat next to her and tried my best to be one of the cool kids in front of this admired girl.

Then one of the boys pulled out a cigarette and lit it. After he took a puff, he passed it to the next person, who took a puff and passed it along. Finally, the cigarette got to me. I had never smoked and didn't know how but wanted to be nonchalant next to my new girlfriend. I took a significant drag on the cigarette and suddenly thought I was about to die. I started coughing and wheezing as I fell backward and then sideways. All the kids started laughing at me, especially the girl I was trying to impress.

My blunders with girls caused me unknown hours of anxiety as a teen. I did not know how to navigate the choppy waters of teenage romance. My experiences did not give me joy; I was dissatisfied with myself because of my inability to form relationships with girls. I wanted to be perceived as unruffled by the girls, but I was anything but unruffled in the end.

As a teenager, I did have something that made me feel special. I sensed I was creative because God gave me insight into scriptures that could bless people's lives. When I thought about sermons, I felt connected to God in ways no other personal outlet provided. Sermon ideas flooded my spirit and intrigued my imagination. I loved the witty and thought-provoking sermons that challenged me to change. That is how I wanted to preach. I had little appreciation for "canned" messages where preachers repeated a lot of dogma and slogans passed down from generation to generation in the church. I was stimulated by preaching that showed intriguing organization and contained themes related to contemporary cultural issues and trends. The preacher who could do that was a genius. Preaching done well gave me joy.

One day our church visited with an association of other churches in Denver. There, one of the pastors brought the sermon. I was not impressed with this preacher's inability to capture my attention, let alone my imagination, as a teen. He wandered through his message without dealing with the Scripture. Then he finished his sermon with a gimmicky closing that riled up the crowd. They went into a frenzy as he took his seat.

About a year later, I was in another church gathering, and this same preacher was on the program to bring the message. He mishandled the Scripture in the same way and told jokes about ministry and the church for about twenty minutes. Then he closed his sermon the exact way he had before.

Once again, the congregation was in a frenzy, but in my teenage assessment, I was flabbergasted. His preaching seemed to be a gimmick. To me, there had to be more to preaching than what this preacher delivered the two times I'd heard him.

While in high school, I read five to ten sermons every weekday as I rode the bus to and from work. My father had a collection of radio sermons that were printed into little booklets for mass distribution, and I had free access to them. The bus ride was about twenty minutes long, which was just enough time to read one sermon, and if I felt like it on the way home, I would read another one. Most of my teen joy came from reading sermons and gleaning what connected with me and what I thought would connect with other people.

In my senior year at George Washington High School in Denver, I was in the Future Business Leaders of America, and during their statewide meeting, they had a speaking contest that I entered and won. Because I won that competition, the teacher who supervised the program recommended to the principal that I speak at my high school graduation. Even though I was an academically struggling

**Dewey Williams at age eighteen, as a young
preacher and a freshman college student.**

student, the idea was approved, and I spoke at graduation in front of
888 graduates. Oddly, I remember the program indicated 444 males
and 444 females in my graduating class. Their family and friends
were also there, as well as the school board administrators, teachers, and staff from George Washington High School. Graduation
took place at the Denver Coliseum, and though I don't know how
many people were there all told, the coliseum—with a capacity of ten
thousand—was nearly full.

I was an eighteen-year-old kid, born in a small town in Iowa,
speaking to thousands of people at a coliseum in a major city in the
United States. I was proud of myself and felt the world held great
possibilities. I wish I had kept a copy of that speech. I remember

talking about staying positive in life as a key to overcoming odds. I barely graduated from high school because of poor grades, but I stood flat footed and pontificated as if I were a wise sage on what it took to be successful.

I had applied to only one college—Bishop College in Dallas, Texas. Bishop College was a HBCU (Historically Black Colleges and Universities). These were schools established before civil rights laws were enacted. These schools gave Blacks the right to go for higher education when going to White schools was denied during slavery and segregation. Despite my poor grades, Bishop College accepted me, but I did not have a clue as to next steps.

The idea that education would help me make something of myself swirled in my head. I was excited about venturing away from home to a college in a city I had only visited once. I don't know why I wasn't scared of the many possible things that could go wrong, but I wasn't. I caught a cab from Dallas Love Field to the campus of Bishop College, not having a clue as to where I needed to go. The security gate attendant directed me to the J.J. Rhoads Education Building, telling me someone there would be able to help me. I was then referred to the men's dormitory and advised to check in. Then I would return to register for classes the next day. I met my roommate, George Castro. I think he was the only Latin student on the campus. We were both quiet, trying to figure out what we needed to do as first-year students, but he had to have a lot of bravery staying on campus at a historically Black college. We never talked about that.

I had arrived with all my possessions in one trunk and one briefcase. I knew Bishop College was going to make something of me.

Perhaps my joy at that time was wrapped in youthful arrogance or youthful naivete. Whatever it was, I was moving to "Big D" (as Dallas was called) to stake my claim as a preacher. I was going to do more than my father ever did. I was going to do ministry in a more significant way. What a load of manure I was full of at eighteen years old—but that load of manure provided joy masked in expectations.

SIX

Joy in Lockup?

After months of weekly trips to Central Prison, I was no longer nervous about visiting Death Row. But I did worry about who would come back to our small group meetings and whether they would openly write down their feelings and stories in that setting. The first time I'd asked them to write in a larger group setting, it was a disaster. Previously, I had hoped the group of twenty-five would benefit from the cathartic process of putting personal thoughts on paper, and I'd also hoped they'd be willing to share their ideas. But I didn't present my hopes well and gave them too many prompts to choose from. We only had fifteen minutes to write. Only a few men wrote anything.

Now that we were working in small groups, things were going much more smoothly. Each time I would bring several sermon quotes with me, and now we were focusing on one question at a time. As usual, we had an officer watching over us.

In this particular meeting, the men and I discussed the story of Paul and Silas singing in chains inside jail as the others listened. We contemplated how Christian joy signifies God intentionally working in our lives. Paul and Silas illustrated this with songs and prayers in a time when they had no idea when or if their adversity would end. We also discussed how people have many forms of incarceration: They're locked in their thoughts, their geography, their relationships, debt, addiction, and more.

We pondered a tough question: "Can there be joy in lockup?" I worried they might be angry when I asked it, and I wasn't sure they would share their innermost ideas about joy. Instead, the question surprised them. They could answer it with great ease, like a student who studied for a calculus test but was asked to solve a simple arithmetic problem. They were expecting contemplation of more difficult matters. Almost all the men gave resounding positive affirmations: "Yes, there is joy in lockup!"

You would expect the residents of Death Row to cry out that their circumstances prevent them from experiencing joy, yet they testified to experiencing joy despite their failings and societal alienation. Joy had come to them through God's prompting.

As I had been with these worshipers to preach and with the Short Journey program, we had formed a bond. Perhaps they felt a real connection to me because my sermons spoke to where they lived, and they realized my goal was not to evangelize them into heaven. The men and I both longed for this bond, and it formed the foundation upon which we built a mutual trust.

While they wrote on the paper I brought with me from outside, they wrote from a secluded residence, a place designed to rob the human spirit of positive expectations. These Christians expressed joy that superseded Death Row's numbing and debilitating approach. The state had judged them, and while a few had hope in the appeals process, they could not turn back time on their sentencing or their actions. Still, joy persisted!

Tenderness and Roughness

When I first met George Thomas Wilkerson, he'd been incarcerated on Death Row for more than a decade, but he was only thirty-five years old. Though the Department of Correction listed him as White, I believed he was of mixed ethnicity. He was one of the brightest people I had ever met. He was not timid to speak up when he had an idea, and he was courteous and respectful to others when they shared theirs. He asked probing questions and responded with penetrating comments. He has been featured several times in the Marshall Project, an online news organization dedicated to covering the US criminal justice system.

George was indicted for the first-degree murder of two victims. He was also indicted for first-degree burglary. In 2006 he was tried and convicted of both counts of first-degree murder based on "malice, premeditation, and deliberation and also under the felony murder rule."[9]

In his writings, George described the difference between human joy and divine joy and compared being "imprisoned by nonphysical things: drug addiction, anger, pride" to "the pure joy that only comes from God" (see fig. 6.1). He expressed that Death Row steals humanity via alienation, and I noticed that he intentionally sought to strengthen relationships within the group. As I only saw the men inside the community room, I had no idea how they interacted in their PODs. However, like me, they sensed his solid theological knowledge and looked to him as their "in-house scholar." He treated them as equals and valued their thoughts, and they respected him.

George surrendered his life to God through faith in Jesus Christ after his sentencing. He contrasted his selfish joy before this transformation to his present, when joy flowed through relationships with other men who'd been incarcerated and with correctional staff on Death Row.

It reminded me of the writings of C. S. Lewis, one of the most influential theologians and authors of the twentieth century (best known for The Chronicles of Narnia). Lewis shared a marvelous

I think there is no simple answer to this question, although based on Scripture and personal experience, I'd say it's definitely possible to be joy-filled despite one's physical incarceration. Joy is a fruit of the Spirit, so I of course mean this in regards to Christians.

Before I was a Christian, I had joy too, but I wasn't physically incarcerated. Although, I also believe that even before I "came to Christ" God was already working in me — hence my joyful disposition. It (joy) is part of who I am, a prominent personality trait.

I have also been imprisoned by nonphysical things: drug addiction, anger, pride. When in chains to these, I still had a measure of joy, but joy wasn't the dominant characteristic. Specifically, with addiction, I was chasing a type of pleasure I thought was the ideal, a euphoria or bliss derived from chemicals. I was enslaved by it. Even as I attained a momentary euphoria, I was living in hell, deprived of the pure Joy that only comes from God.

Story

Before coming to prison, I was imprisoned by pride. I was so concerned about my reputation, about what others thought of me, that I felt forced to do things I didn't want to do. I was anxious all the time, worried, afraid — constantly visualizing all these scenarios where I'd have to fight someone because of some perceived slight. I was miserable and high-strung. Pride stole my joy, it muffled it, it ~~redu~~ diminished my personality. Pride dehumanized me, and moved me to dehumanize others. Pride objectified me, and others, as it distorted my perception of reality. Over the years, as I go to war against my pride, I find my joy quotient increasing inversly proportionate to my decreasing pride. Maybe one day I can embrace being nothing, embrace true humility.

Prison presents plenty of obstacles to joy, by nature I think. I have a working theory that a person cannot be fully human ~~so~~ while alienated from others. God created us as individuals with unique personalities, but He also designed us to be part of ~~s~~ collectives: marriage, family, communities, etc.

It is through the ~~various~~ various relationship dynamics my humanity finds full expression. For example, I can be tender with my mom or sister in a way I cannot with others, while I can be rough and blunt with my brothers in a way I can't with others. Both, tenderness and roughness, are parts of me I cannot express outside a relationship. Thus, when I can't fully express my humanity, I feel incomplete, oppressed, deprived of joy. God promises to give us life abundant, and I believe He's referring to enabling us to fully express our humanity. Within moral boundaries, of course. Joy is directly influenced by my ability to be fully human. Prison is highly effective at creating barriers to relationships. I have so many joy-filled moments Joy, like I said, is part of my disposition, so when I say I had a joy-filled moment, I'm referring

to a particular intensity of joy.
The ones that come to mind are
when I have these moments of
AWARENESS, of understanding
the reality of my faith:
   —That God is real and loves me.
   — That He chose me, a sinner,
      saved me, and walks with me
      daily.
   — that I am truly blessed.
   — that Life itself, the mere fact
      I exist and know it is mira-
      culous.
   — that I get to participate in
      creation, and work with God
      at shaping Eternity.
All these truths and more sometimes puncture my day-to-day
train of thought, and I am in an
ecstasy of Awe, wonder, and joy.

Figure 6.1. Response from George Thomas Wilkerson

understanding of how God utilizes joy when he wrote, "Joy is the serious business of Heaven."[10] While human awareness and engagement in joy is beneficial, initiation and ownership of joy does not belong to us. Joy is God's business and God's gift to humanity.

George's response also reminds us that "joy is a fruit of the Spirit." Many people consider other virtues to be more important and impactful than joy. Joy is shrunken beneath other spiritual fruit: often love, peace, forgiveness, and patience. People consider joy whimsical or spontaneous and feel we are blessed only when joy's winds blow in our direction.

I refute the notion that joy is a lesser virtue or weaker than the power of negativity. Joy persists through our personal misdeeds, through failings of the judicial system, through racial injustices, and even through attempts to take lives via lethal injection. Joy calls us to live in heavenly pursuit.

Joy on Death Row by George Thomas Wilkerson

George is an avid writer and a skilled artist. He painted about joy on Death Row as a gift for me, but he couldn't give me the canvas because of rules forbidding exchanges of items between those who are incarcerated and those who volunteer.

George presented his drug addiction before knowing Christ as a broken joy, a joy derived from the sensation narcotics can give. I've never been a drug user, but my joy before this Death Row experience was also broken. My addiction was a desire for notoriety and status. I feigned success and security when I felt anything but. George helped me see how my desires drew me away from God.

The Armor of God

I already introduced you to Fernando Garcia, who was six feet tall and middle aged when we met. He worked out, and it showed. Although he was large and muscular, he was also mild mannered. After I got to know him, he admitted he considered himself to be less literate than the other men who had taken writing classes in prison. Even so, his writings were substantive and heartfelt.

He wrote about running away from God in "street life," even while God was pursuing him (see fig. 6.2). Before prison and Death Row he was too busy to listen to God. But according to his writing, he felt the presence of the Holy Spirit. Fernando helped me look at my own busyness and how it distanced me from God.

When I visited Central Prison later in 2019, Fernando couldn't meet. He came to me breathless and sweaty to let me know it was his outdoor hour. He wanted to play basketball. I was disappointed not to spend more time with this powerful writer, but I certainly understood. The men were only able to go outside for one hour per week to experience the sky, the wind, the rain, or the snow.

Many people think joy is a whimsical experience whereby karma or fate directs joy to fix problems or to resolve tensions. Instead, I believe joy is on a campaign to intervene in our lives. Joy pushes against the forces attempting to derail us physically, emotionally, and spiritually. Joy propels us toward love, righteousness, justice, and

Yes. Joy is not a feeling, but a spiritual fruit of the Holy Spirit. Joy can be expressed in many forms in any circumstances & situations. Just look at the life of Daniel. Even though he was locked into slavery he had "joy" because he was a man led by the Holy Spirit. Joy come because of the intimate fellowship in God, and how He is with His people, in His Consiston constant faithfulness & His truth. Everything we experience has to go through God's hands. We can cross reference that with the 1st chpt of Job, & the life of Joseph God's blueprint for their life was already written out. We having faith, & trust in God helps us to have joy in life no matter the circumstances.

STORY:

I guess, I can start this story with the fact that as I was being pursued by God to come back to Him. I was running away more and more, further and further from Him. I was trying to find myself. I was being reared by drug dealers who grew grew-up with my father. So to them I was part of their family. I was able to be part of many a things that I wish I did not see or be part of! Street life was hard! Street life had it's own rules & leaders. And I being into the life via family friends I was not able to be in contact with God on a personal level because I was in a realm that God did not like to visit. A realm in which God tried to pull people out of. But I was too busy to listen to God or see what God's plan was for me. I did not have joy when doing me. only when I gave myself to God did I truely find joy and myself.

I believe that it is difficult to have Joy when faced with the many distractions in life. When I take my focus off of God, my life become CHAOS. When I don't PRAY in the quiet times in the morning before we have our cells opened my mornings seem to have plenty of opportunities to go sour? But once I put on the "ARMOR of God", I feel assured after a good prayer that I'm good. I feel the "Holy Spirit upon me. I feel the presence of "the LORD" with me. Then and only then do I experience true joy Because the same way I put on my clothes, I put on Jesus, and everywhere I go Jesus goes also.

As I have said before - "Joy comes in Knowing God." Well may- haps the best moment for me is when I Truely came back to the fold 'Gods way! IT felt like Rushing waters all in my stomach. more powerful then butter-

bliss. A scence of peace in Knowing - OK God has me. As my "adonai" He owns me, He values me He's going to take care of me. It's hard to submitt but it is also exhilinating to Know that with God it is always an adventure. It's always joyous Thinking about God doing a small thing for me. Or helping me do a simple thing for some- one like interceding for somore and watching the prayers get answered.

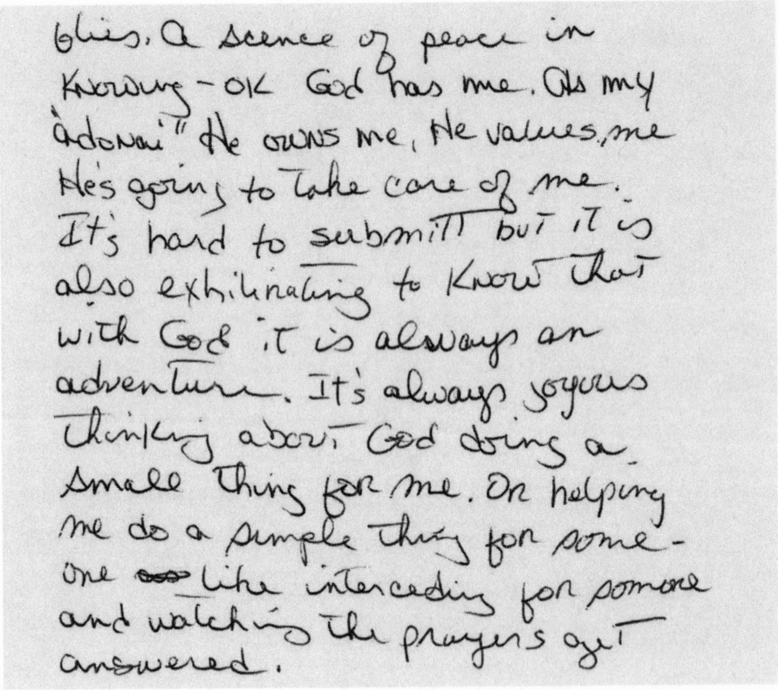

Figure 6.2. Response from Fernando Garcia

hope—right where we are at any moment—even when our environ-ment seems counter to what is good.

In his writing, Fernando recalled from memory the biblical sto-ries of Daniel, Job, and Joseph and how they endured difficulties yet were blessed with joy. These stories fueled Fernando's embrace of God in the hope he would experience final victory in reaching heaven the way the ancient Hebrew personalities did. He desired the end of his story—his last years in prison—to be marked by persistence in the Christian faith and transformation much like Daniel, Job, and

Joseph. Fernando expressed an expectation of God to deliver joy to him as God did for biblical patriarchs more than 2,000 years before.

Nearly all notable biblical figures struggled, and most struggles were grandiose. We might say they were of "biblical proportion." What these Bible heroes and heroines discovered was the existence of God working beneath and behind the surface of events to uncover a brighter outcome.

Anger, despair, envy, and grief may appear to work harder to press on our lives unless we set our minds and hearts against them. Frustration, fear, and guilt are constantly calling us to surrender to the demise unless we shut them out. In our minds, joy is not as evident as the corruption that can bring us down. It is difficult to recognize joy standing up against evil and difficult to express joy when evil's ugliness horrifies our God-given human spirit.

The power of Christian joy is that it forecasts and promises better outcomes even in seasons of misfortune or oppression. In his book *God of the Oppressed*, James H. Cone wrote that Christian proclaimers and theologians have "a language of celebration and joy that the freedom promised is already present in the community's struggle for liberation."[11] For believers on Death Row, their current and ultimate freedom is already present.

Fernando seemed to be living in this freedom. He answered my question about joy in lockup by writing that he felt assured after a good prayer: "The same way I put on my clothes, I put on Jesus, and everywhere I go Jesus goes also."

When we persist in studying the Word of the Bible and making prayer part of our daily routines, joy becomes obstinate in our countenance.

Joy Is Not Man-Made

James Edward Jaynes, a White man, had been on Death Row for about twenty-five years—half his life—when I met him. As of this writing, just over a third of the North Carolina Death Row population is White, 52 of the 135 women and men.[12] Conversely, North Carolina is just under 68 percent White.[13] James was of average build and soft-spoken. While he did not say much verbally, he said plenty in his writing (see fig. 6.3). He was sincere in his desire to participate.

In April 1992 James was tried capitally and found guilty of first-degree murder based on "malice, premeditation, and deliberation" under the felony murder rule.[14] He was originally indicted for murder as well as first-degree arson, first-degree burglary, robbery with a dangerous weapon, and two counts of larceny of an automobile. The jury found James guilty of all charges.

Memory must play a key role in imagining nature for the incarcerated, as they are confined to the indoors for all but one hour per week. They are limited to the nature of their bodies and the people they encounter. Long walks such as those James used to escape an abusive father are not available, so the incarcerated are forced to employ their imaginations for escape.

There is a prevailing idea in our culture that joy only occurs when we take prescribed steps or follow the popular thinking techniques of the day. This is the hope of self-help theorists: Live *our* way and you will prosper intellectually, emotionally, and physically. When we narrow joy down to a man-made circumference, we fail to see its mystery and God's extensive handiwork.

James referenced how difficult it was to be joyful when other residents of Death Row were full of gloom and doom. He wrote,

There is no doubt that JOY can be had in lock-up/prison. I'm able to find Joy in the changing of the seasons, a phone call home or a good book. Even though I'm not where I want to be, I am not miserable, I am not bitter. I'm able to turn on the radio and hear of people that are worse off than myself. I'm not always bubbling with Joy, but it's only a few breaths away.

It's not only possible to lead a Joy-filled existence, it happens every day. Even when I don't feel Joy-ful, I see guys that are. I am not alone, as I have my trust & faith in God, that Heaven awaits.

Storey

When I was a kid my homelife was bad. My Dad was an abusive alcoholic.

To get away from the
situation I would go for
long walks by myself. I
enjoyed walking in the woods,
through fallow fields and
by the creek. I had a few
Places I'd go. I might sit
for an hour in a quiet, moss-
filled place, or the bedrock
of the creek. I felt JOY
in being surrounded by Nature
and being away from home.
I learned to enjoy solitude.

It can be difficult
to always have JOY when
the guy next to you is
blaming the police, the D.A
or God for their circum-
stances. Or someone will
say, "what good is living,
if I never get out of
prison". Negativity can

make things difficult, but I try to keep my mind on positive things, and pray that the particular person finds peace & JOY without ruining mine.

My most memorable JOY-filled moment was back in the early 90's. My Mom and my cousin came to see me here. I knew they were coming to bring Holiday goodies but got the dates mixed up. The day they came was unexpectedly easly and the visit was great. My Mom has since passed away but I still recall how happy & Joy-ful we all three were for those few hours.

Figure 6.3. Response from James Edward Jaynes

"It can be difficult to always have joy when the guy next to you is blaming the police, the DA, or God for their circumstances . . . but I try to keep my mind on positive things, and pray that the particular person finds peace and joy without ruining mine." James handled the negativity of daily life by trusting God.

John Swinton, a Scottish theologian and chair in divinity and religious studies at the School of Divinity, History, Philosophy & Art History at the University of Aberdeen, related a story of teaching a distance-learning course where the discussion involved spiritual experiences. Swinton wrote, "The woman who was deaf, Angela, began to tell us about a dream she'd had. In that dream she had met with Jesus in heaven. She and Jesus talked for some time, and she said she had never experienced such peace and joy. 'Jesus was everything I had hoped he would be,' she said. '*And his signing was amazing!*'"[15]

In Swinton's example, heaven's perfection did not involve healing. Instead, the deaf woman experienced heaven as a place where her social, relational, and communication barriers disappeared. This matches James's experience of joy through the mystery of faith within the belly of Death Row's daily misery. Through his hopeful outlook, faith was activated and eventually realized.

James taught me that we must turn to prayer when we cannot control others or circumstances. I have found that prayer is an aid in finding joy. Prayer can reinforce the idea of God being the ultimate giver of blessings. I try to pray honest prayers, telling God exactly what I am thinking and feeling. These words are not always pleasant, but I feel better when I unleash myself before God. Prayer is part of my healing.

Women's Forgiveness and Joy

The purpose of modern-day prison is to keep unsafe people cordoned away, but the original idea was for criminals to repent and confess. The word *penitentiary* originated in Late Middle English from the Latin word *paenitentia*, meaning repentance. When I visited the only three women on Death Row in 2017, and again in 2020, we talked about repentance and forgiveness.

Unlike the single, foreboding building of Central Prison where the men are held, the North Carolina Correctional Institute for Women is a gated campus consisting of many buildings connected by outdoor paths, each with an ominous fence. It is more cumbersome for a volunteer like me to reach the Death Row incarcerated: more locks and buzzers and metal doors and correctional officers behind thick Plexiglas windows.

As of recently, there were three women on Death Row in North Carolina. I was glad to meet them and expected to make good connections with them. Most of my professional work in public assistance, child welfare, and mental health services has been with women.

As I stepped into Section E, where the women on Death Row lived in March 2020, the tables and chairs for our meeting were placed in the center of the common area. The women wore the women's uniform: a burgundy top and dark blue jeans. The room was large and wide, surrounded by eight cells and two shower stalls. Most daily life happened here. Next to the lockers was a steel vanity table, a mirror, and a telephone where the women could receive—but not make—phone calls.

The three of us and the chaplain sat under the watch of a correctional officer as well as the dual lighting from a bar-covered skylight and fluorescent panels. I was not afforded the opportunity to deliver all five joy sermons to the women as I did with the men, so I hoped each of us might take turns reading my sermon "Incarcerated Joy." One of the women declined, so I read the sermon aloud myself. The primary point I made in the sermon was that there are many types of prisons people build for themselves—debt, addiction, and destructive relationships among them. Of course, these women were locked in prison awaiting death, so we focused on the Bible story of Paul and Silas praying and singing in prison in the book of Acts and how there is a special spiritual power when people pray and sing together. Paul and Silas and the other people incarcerated with them had joy even in the face of adversity. They were willing to worship together, even if it meant their lives. In the story, their joy literally shook the prison.

I was taken with the women's responses, especially by their ideas of forgiveness and community. You see, these three spent 100 percent of their time with one another, meaning their thoughts about forgiveness and community were very personal.

We talked as a group about how the three women were reliant on one another. They had little or no access to other in-person relationships. When they felt down, they lifted one another up. When they were sick, they were nursemaids to one another. As I sat with them, I praised God that these women had one another to lean on. Like Paul and Silas, they had a special spiritual power when they prayed and sang together.

God's presence brought me joy in the lowest seasons of my life, and I believe God played a role in my opportunity to uncover joy with these people who awaited their execution. If these men and women could experience joy in lockup, and if I could find joy through them, I believe joy is available—wherever and in whatever circumstances—to all who avail the presence of God.

SEVEN

Anger and Joy

In my years serving in prisons, I've witnessed much debilitating anger. Anger prohibits wards of the State from living in the current day because they cannot move past a former experience. One man expressed such fierce anger toward his ex-girlfriend's betrayal that he admitted to considering violence against her when he got out. Another man talked about anger toward the police, the prosecutor, his public defender, and the judge because he believed there was a conspiracy to convict him.

I don't mean to say I witnessed physical outbursts. When groups like mine visited, it was a special privilege, and the men and women respected the opportunity. What I did find was that when they discussed their anger about ending up in prison or their resentment to God for their situation, they often broke down and admitted to being angry with themselves.

Many of the incarcerated who serve time in Gen Pop (General Population, where most incarcerated are housed) tend to hold on to their anger longer because they have hope of getting out. Some plan to get even or prove to the world they are not bad. When living on the

Row, there is no hope for a future back with others. These incarcerated must learn to manage their anger in different ways. Otherwise, it's locked away with them.

Before Paul and Silas were locked up in the dungeon of the Philippian jail, they had delivered a slave woman from the control of her slaveholder. This slave woman was valuable because she was believed to be a fortune teller. After Paul exorcised the demons, her financial value was diminished. Her owners became angry. They sued Paul and Silas, had them arrested, and tossed them into Philippi's dungeon. The sermon I used captured the anger of the slave owners, but it also dealt with a fundamental emotion that runs deep in the human experience and especially in the realm of incarceration: anger.

Of all our emotions, anger fires up the fastest. It alters our thinking and behaviors in a flash. We all hold anger in our brains and bodies. Its root could stem from a mean comment by a peer in fifth grade, the jealousy of a colleague, or a time we were misunderstood by someone we care about. Anger's grip can cause us to lose sight of our internal moral compass. Neuroscientist Giovanni Frazzetto wrote, "Anger exemplifies the irrepressible vigour of the emotions. It puts our judgement to the test, forcing us to consider how to behave in frustrating circumstances, respond adequately to offence, and decide on the best action. Anger is entangled with choice. Feeling anger raises questions of values and options, and thus of ethics, morality and conduct."[16]

I must stop here because anger is often the emotion of both crime victims and the State. It is anger that seeks an eye for an eye, and it is anger that desires to retaliate. My mother used to say, "If someone does you wrong, and you get even, what does that make you?" Her point was that getting even makes you a wrongdoer. When the State allows anger and outrage to allow retaliation by taking someone's life, it destroys our human values. I believe this retributive type of justice—the death penalty—is ethical and moral hypocrisy.

When I started these months of small groups, I asked the men to respond to my sermon quotes in writing. I laid out ten questions or quotes and asked them to pick the one they wanted to write about. After several visits, I noticed that none of them had picked the anger quote. Why? Was my sermon inaccurate or untruthful? Did it have a cultural component they couldn't relate to? Or was anger simply a topic the men hoped to avoid?

Anger was rarely expressed by those who came to worship or write. The general tenor was upbeat, filled with smiles and laughter about the opportunity to pull away from daily routines. It was a rare occasion if someone showed up with negative emotions. There were times when men said they were drained, feeling defeated, or worried about their family. Not one of them ever said they were angry.

The men's reluctance to write about their anger is consistent with common human tendencies to camouflage negative emotions. Often people present as happy when they are miserable. They don't want to be known as a complainer, or they think others don't care or can't manage negative expressions. The frequent thought is that anger is not Christlike, so especially within Christian circles, there's often a masking of dark emotions.

Some words taken from the lips of Jesus equate anger with murder. Jesus said, "Whoever murders shall be liable to judgment," and "If you are angry with a brother or sister, you will be liable to judgment" (Matthew 5:21–22). What are those convicted of murder to think if Jesus held anger in the same light as murder? The emphasis of Jesus's teaching is not to have people deny their anger but to know that anger must be taken as seriously as murder.

On this day I sat with four men and gave the anger sermon quote as the only option. After the men wrote their responses, we talked about anger. The consensus was that anger was a universal experience for men on Death Row. They struggled with addressing anger because it never went away. Victims' families were angry at them for the lives they were convicted of taking. Prosecutors and the courts seemed angry with them on behalf of society. The families of the men were angry because of the decisions they made leading to Death Row. The men were angry at the parents and family members who failed them throughout their lives as well as the public defenders who failed to represent them well. But most significantly, the men were angry at themselves—angry about what they did and where they ended up.

When you put a group of angry individuals together for an extended time, anger has an overflow effect. The men were drowning in it.

It is not a sin to be angry. I did not suggest the men denounce feelings of anger. I suggested they not allow anger to rule their behaviors because anger would not solve their situation.

Energy That Produces Chaos

One of my earliest and fondest memories of Richard Warner was on my first day of visiting Death Row with Short Journey. He introduced himself with a broad smile and said, "We are glad you guys came to be with us."

He believed anger produced chaos. He wrote, "When anger governs, it leads to bitterness . . . and to have such negative emotions can cause serious problems in one's life." Richard captured the essence of the problem of allowing anger to be your primary driving force when he argued that chaos is the by-product. Quite often chaos leads people to greater conflict or to withdraw from having contact or interactions with the angry person. Unless your aim is conflict, anger does not ameliorate that which is making you angry.

Not only is anger a short-term disruptor to joy, but it can also cause awful feelings and consequences for years. Sustained anger jeopardizes spiritual, psychosocial, and even physical well-being.

In Richard's words, you can feel the spiraling effect of being trapped in anger's snare. For years he maintained harsh feelings about his father, and he believed his anger contributed to his use of and addiction to substances—an addiction that cycled around and further heightened his feelings of anger. Richard's anger started as an immediate response to his father's failings, but it turned into a decades-long harboring of negative feelings.

Richard described how his anger turned into a major thief in his life, writing, "I trashed [my father's] home and costed thousands of dollars in damages. My angry choices caused a divide between me and my father that has not been closed to this day. I don't find joy in my action/choices, and or the consequences from that anger." His angry response drove a deeper wedge between himself and his father. Richard was on Death Row with limited options to make things better, and his father had expressed no desire to mend the divide.

What happened between him and his father was heartbreaking—especially how they ended up with a lasting separation. But hallelujah! God intervened in Richard's life and brought joy to him. In the face of all the negative outcomes, Richard made peace within himself, leading to anger release. He began to live a new way through the joy that comes from knowing Jesus Christ. Out of the sadness of Richard's story, we get a glimmer of hope.

Where Richard had out-of-control anger that crippled his relationships and drove him to substance abuse and crime, my anger has been more of a "grin and bear it" type. Instead, I pretend to be okay as I stew in resentment.

Most of my own resentment is internalized and based on my inability to fix problems. I resented God for not giving me more of what I thought I needed to be a successful person.

Richard's fix for anger was a relationship with God through Christ Jesus. Same here.

Writing prompt for those who are incarcerated:

We must be careful to not allow anger to rule as the governing emotion as we make our life choices. Anger will mess you up and mess somebody else up. When anger governs, it usually just makes you feel bad and makes things worse.

Never Let Anger Rule

Anger may give you a momentary "win" over someone else. When such wins are for personal gain, you push your way around—but is it worth the harsh feelings created?

Jim McCloskey, former prison chaplain and founder of Centurion Ministries, the first group in America devoted to over-turning wrongful convictions, discussed anger entrapment in his book, *When Truth Is All You Have*. He wrote:

> One of the most astounding things I experience when I talk to our exonerees is how many of them have managed to get rid of the deep, all-consuming anger that possessed them when they were wrongly convicted. And how many of them say the same thing: that the anger is another prison, binding

them to those who conspired against them; that to be truly free meant more than walking beyond the prison walls, that it also required walking beyond the walls of that rage.[17]

While it is true that people can manipulate you using anger, it is also true that anger can control you. You can follow every law in your city and country, but anger can still imprison you.

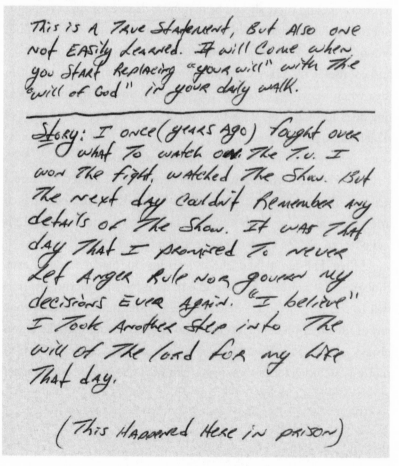

This is A True Statement, But Also one not EASily Learned. It will Come when you Start Replacing "your will" with The "will of God" in your daily walk.

Story: I once (years Ago) fought over what To watch on The T.v. I won The fight, watched The Show. But The next day couldn't Remember any details of The Show. It was That day That I promised To never Let Anger Rule Nor govern my decisions Ever Again. "I believe" I Took Another Step into The will of The lord for my life That day.

(This Happened Here in prison)

Figure 7.1. Response from Alden Harden

What follows is a story recounted by Alden Harden (see fig. 7.1). He described a heated moment about something as mundane as what to watch on TV. In his anger he prevailed, but his anger created such internal emotional mayhem that he could not enjoy the program or remember it. Anger robbed him of the moment.

Often, we find ourselves angry about insignificant matters—or "making a mountain out of a molehill," as they say. There are degrees to problems, and there should be matching degrees of anger responding to horrible problems. It's problematic when a person has minor emotions of anger to major problems and vice versa. Author, speaker, and counselor Dr. Gary Chapman provided a good summary of this idea when he wrote, "To have the same response to minor issues as one does for major issues is to mismanage one's anger."[18] A part of Alden Harden's spiritual maturity was to learn to lay aside expressions of anger over minor or insignificant matters.

I felt blessed when I was in the presence of Alden because I realized him to be one of the men on Death Row who encouraged attendance at the worship services. He was known to encourage his sad peers to look to God and to keep the faith.

Alden Harden talked about learning to manage anger, even though it was not easy. He was able to do it by surrendering his self-will to the will of God. I believe Alden wrote more responses than any of the other men. He just kept showing up. Looking back, he was always upbeat. It is hard to imagine him as angry. I view his testimony as an indicator of a changed man who was once prone to anger and is now prone to joy.

EIGHT

The Crippling of My Joy

M y young adult years were filled with a mixture of extremely good times and extremely bad times. I guess Charles Dickens predicted my young adult life when he said, "It was the best of times, it was the worst of times."[19] I have so many fond memories filled with blessings and excited moments of personal, family, and community joy. I cannot count or list all the good and joy-filled times that happened to me during these years, but I will name some of them.

After I got to Bishop College in Dallas, Texas, I began studying religion and philosophy. What a fantastic time in my life. I went from a setting where I saw and knew very few Black people with a PhD to a situation where every weekday, and sometimes on the weekends, I was dealing with Black intellectuals with doctorates. Having barely graduated from high school, I was a student who lacked academic training. (I had to beg a teacher to give me a passing grade at the end of my senior year so I could graduate.) My GPA entering college was 2.0, but now I was on a campus where scholarly excellence was advertised as the pathway to positive individual and community outcomes.

On top of that, Bishop College was a magnet school for Black Preachers in the United States. When I first matriculated, it was estimated that more Black preachers were studying at Bishop College than at any other college, university, or seminary campus in the nation. Every major city in the United States, from coast to coast, had Bishop College alumni pastoring in large churches. I was surrounded by other young Black preachers daily and was exposed to many Black Church practices I had never seen or imagined. I was learning academics, but I was also learning about the diverse systems within the Black Church that were different from my personal experience in the storefront congregation I grew up in.

But early on, I had to admit that I did not know how to study. Every first-year student at Bishop College had to take a freshman orientation class. One of the required books was *On Becoming an Educated Person* by Virginia Voeks—a book designed for a person like myself who needed to learn and understand what it takes to be a good student. This book did not resolve all my study deficits, but it gave me helpful recommendations to follow. Some administrators or professors at Bishop College knew that some of us would come there lacking study skills and would need help. That was a part of Bishop College's legacy. Professors cared about helping those of us with Black heritage rise even when our circumstances had not nurtured us the best.

On top of that, I applied to and was accepted into the legendary Bishop College Concert Choir under the leadership of the renowned Dr. J. Harrison Wilson. This choir rehearsed four days a week and sang once a week in the chapel. We also traveled, and I was permitted to go on trips representing the college in many cities across the nation. I was not a trained vocal musician, but I was able to carry a tune and learned how to read music well enough as a baritone to make it into the choir.

In my first year of college, I learned more about music than I had learned in my whole life. During one rehearsal, Dr. Wilson, who seemed to enjoy challenging young preachers to do better, explained we were going to learn the Litany of the Saints—part of a chant sung during the processional of cardinals in the Vatican when a new pope is elected. Dr. Wilson stopped his explanation of the song and, in front of the whole choir, asked me, "What is a cardinal?" I did not know how a cardinal was related to the church, so I responded, "Somebody playing for Saint Louis." The whole choir laughed as Dr. Wilson sighed and threw his hands in the air in disgust. That exposure in the Bishop College Concert Choir broadened my appreciation of church music and all music outside the confines of my humble and limited background. I learned about the hard work that went into musical excellence.

The crowning joy from my young adult life was getting to know and then marrying Lynne Rochelle McGraw while attending Bishop College. Lynne, like myself, was a freshman in 1973. She also was from Denver, but as teenagers, we went to different high schools and churches, so we did not know each other well. I knew *of* her because she was a teenage pianist who played at her church and high school. She continually rebuffs my words when I tell people I didn't know her; I just knew her fame when we were teenagers. Lynne was and still is a gifted musician.

Lynne knew music. She probably could have taught her music theory class as a freshman. The music professors recognized that she already knew much of their teaching as a first-year student. She had perfect pitch, read music well, and played gospel music by ear. To top it off, Lynne was an excellent academic student who graduated with honors from high school and could have picked from various colleges or universities. She chose Bishop primarily because of the famed concert choir, which had come to her church in Denver to sing routinely. For some mysterious reason she liked me, and we became running buddies, then romantic mates, then an engaged couple, and then newlyweds. The one constant good in my young adult life was Lynne. She was the heart of my joy as a young man.

Adding to the good in my young adult years was the arrival of two daughters, Charity and Tiffany, when I was twenty-one and twenty-three years old respectively. I came from a family of eight children and had always valued family life. In my childhood, we

Dewey Williams and Lynne: young, in love, and engaged at nineteen.

**Lynne and Dewey Williams with Tiffany, age
ten months, and Charity, age three.**

enjoyed living at home. Even though we did not have much in terms
of material possessions, we had family joy sitting around listening to
James Cleveland's gospel albums, learning the harmonies, and imi-
tating the soloist from his great recorded hits.

As an adult I wanted to duplicate what my parents had provided
to my siblings and me. I wanted to have many kids who would be
given laughter and love. Lynne and I only had two girls, but these
two girls were jam-packed with laughter, love, energy, and intrigue.
All of that is code language to say we had our hands full, but we loved
it because they added joy.

As a young adult, I had much good happening, but the good mingled with the bad during these years. And when I was twenty-one,

an event shook me to my core. Suddenly the person who most motivated me could no longer be my rock of consistency. My joy was truly crippled.

Tragedy Strikes

I was not at the family home on Oneida Street in Denver on August 6, 1976, when my sister Genevieve murdered my father in cold blood and attempted to kill my mother. I was away at college in Dallas, trying to learn how to be a preacher like my dad.

It was the start of my junior year, and I was focused on what I had to do for work and school. I wasn't tuned in to national news or politics, even though it was an election year. (Carter succeeded Ford that November.) I was big into sports, though, and it was easy to get me in conversation about the Denver Broncos. I was very excited about Denver basketball too. Our hometown team, which had recently switched from the Denver Rockets to the Denver Nuggets, joined the NBA (from the ABA) that year.

I had started preaching when I was a teenager, and now I was following my lifelong dream. My joy at the time was like a soaring kite, riding on the hope of the education carrying me to new heights.

It was a Friday evening, and I remember feeling good. I had already married Lynne, and we were very happy as married students. Lynne was five months along with our first child. We had positive prospects for our future.

Lynne and I came home around nine o'clock. We had both been busy all week. It was the end of the day, and I was looking forward to lying down.

Then the phone rang. It was my younger sister, Patricia. I answered the phone, and she said, "I've been trying to call you all day." There was panic in her voice when she blurted out the news: "Genevieve shot Dad." Initially, I thought she said Genevieve was shot dead. I was confused. Who would want to hurt my sister? Then she explained it to me again. It was a shock.

This call had startled me out of nowhere, bringing news that my dad was gone and my sister had taken his life.

I didn't know what to do with myself. I didn't know how to respond. This was so extremely out of bounds in terms of what I expected. What was supposed to happen with my dad, my family, and me? I was stunned. I stared at the brown corded phone, then sat down on the bed and called Lynne to come in from our tiny kitchen. She was devasted and stunned as well. We were mixed up. Genevieve a killer? To that point, we had considered her the angel in our family.

***

My dad, Rev. Granville M. Williams, had started Holy Spirit Missionary Baptist Church. For the first year, the church operated out of our home. It is still in existence. He was also on staff at the Denver Public Schools. He worked as a janitor at Manual High School and spent part of his day in a booth in the parking lot. He monitored students and staff coming and going and made sure everybody who was there was supposed to be. He liked it because he got to know a lot of people, do a lot of reading, and prepare his sermons as he monitored the lot.

My father was the son of a miner from West Virginia, and his parents died when he was a teen. He and his ten sisters and brothers were fostered out to family and friends in the Des Moines area. During World War II he served in the Medical Corps at Shepherd

Field near Wichita Falls, Texas. In 1945 he entered the Open Bible College in Des Moines where he studied under the GI Bill.[20]

Dad was just over six feet tall with an average build. He typically dressed in a suit and tie but would wear dress pants when he was being casual. He wore wire-framed glasses and was always clean shaven. I never saw him in gym shoes. The only time I recall seeing my father presenting as someone other than a preacher was when he was getting cleaned up. He had a chiseled jaw with dimples and a wide smile. His hands were large enough to swallow my hands within them. He believed in a firm handshake as an indicator of strong character.

As kids we would often laugh at people we thought were odd or unusual, but our dad would scold us for it. He was soft-spoken, and

Reverend Granville M. Williams, Dewey Williams's
father, standing as pastor in the pulpit of the St. John
Baptist Church in Mason City, Iowa, circa 1960.

he stood flat-footed and preached without a lot of showmanship. His sermons did not include a tune, customary in Black churches, where ministers will add a little musical flavor and flamboyance to their message. He was stoic when dealing with problems or when contemplating matters. He did not engage in arguments or try to prove his point over someone else's logic.

One of my favorite memories with Dad was when I alone accompanied him to a state meeting in Iowa, about a two-hour drive from our home in Des Moines. I rarely had one-on-one time with my dad, so this trip sticks out. Usually, when I got up in the morning, he was already gone. He worked hard, and there was little idle time to enjoy. Also, my mother, Willie—whom we all called "Mother"—was usually with us, plus two to four other kids. On this day we sat side by side, listening to the AM radio news or religious programming and maybe some Paul Harvey. Dad got a chuckle out of the way Paul Harvey would say things. It was probably 1965 or 1966, so I would have been about ten years old. On our ride back, we stopped for ice cream at an old-fashioned place. I cherish the memory to this day.

Our home was like the Grand Central Station of the neighborhood, both in Des Moines and Denver. Our mother saw her home as her mission field. While I wanted simply to have friends over to play, she would ask everyone if they knew Jesus.

* * *

The day of the family tragedy, my parents were returning from Vacation Bible School. It was early afternoon. There were eight children in the station wagon with them, including my niece Crystal and nephew Melvin who half grew up with us in the house on Oneida Street. Though I was off at college, and though my oldest siblings,

Granville and Dean, were living elsewhere, most of my siblings were living in Denver at the time.

The house was about five minutes from Stapleton International Airport, which has since been replaced by Denver International Airport. Our home sat a few blocks from one of the main runways where jumbo aircraft would take off and land. We regularly heard the booming sound of airplane jet engines, and from our backyard at night, we could see the lights in the main cabin of each plane as it neared touchdown.

Dad was in the driver's seat of his red Chevrolet Impala station wagon, pulling up into the yard. The wagon wasn't new, but it was new to him. My nephew Melvin was in the third row. His mother—my sister Gladys, whom he called "Ma"—was waiting inside for the family to come home for lunch. My parents played a big part in raising him, and because of that, he called my parents "Dad" and "Mother". What follows is what Melvin remembers of the fateful day. He was ten years old at the time.

> It was August, it was summertime, the station wagon windows were down. Genevieve was sitting on the porch. I remember sticking my head out the car window and saying, "Hi Genevieve." I was really happy to see her. She had a blank look on her face. She walked up to the car. Dad said, "Hello, Genevieve," in his fatherly way. She had a black purse, and she reached into the purse and pulled out the gun and shot the side of his temple. Then, she reached in the car right by his face and shot at Mother, but that bullet missed.
>
> I remember Mother saying, "Oh Granville."
>
> His head was slumped down, and the car hit the house in a slow roll. All the kids jumped out. It was a carload of

kids. There was blood coming out of his head and he was slobbering. He wore sky-blue double Swedish knit pants and a white shirt, the style of the day.

The ambulance came, and the paramedics threw him on the stretcher. Somebody said, "He's still alive." Crystal went in the house to get a bunch of knives and tried to stab Genevieve. I was stunned. Crystal was zapping out. She was just a little kid.

I couldn't believe what I was looking at. I just remember thinking, Wow, like, that was my man. Dad was my man. I did everything with him. He was the real deal, he really was.

Ma grabbed Genevieve by the wrist and pointed the gun toward the ground. Genevieve just stood there. Wasn't no fight, she just put it down. She didn't move, no facial expression, nothing.

I have tried to imagine the inside of the station wagon. The blood and gore must have been horrific. I can imagine the wails of my mother, niece, and nephew. I find it harder to imagine the look on my sister's face as she held the gun. I do not know the names or whereabouts of the other kids in the back of the station wagon.

I can't imagine being a little kid and witnessing such a thing. It must have been traumatizing and devastating—something they carry to this day.

My sister was arrested.[21] She went to Denver City Jail without bond but was later put in a hospital. She never went to prison.

Dad was put on life support, and the staff of Denver General Hospital attempted to save him.[22] My older brother Marvin said there were tubes and wires all over Dad's hospital bed. My brother Stanley grabbed Dad's toe and squeezed it to generate a response. There was none. We were all heartbroken.

Surely there was anger as well, though Mother tried her best to quell it. Mother and Dad taught us anger is a cage you get trapped in. I remember them citing Paul's letters to the Ephesians: "Be angry but do not sin; do not let the sun go down on your anger" (4:26). Our parents tried to keep us from actions leading to sin. For example, they had zero toleration for alcohol as it led to drunkenness. There was no card playing, which could lead to gambling. Dancing led to sexually inappropriate behavior and promiscuity. That's the way they thought and taught us.

After they took Dad off life support, my older brother hit Genevieve's husband, Lloyd. The police were called to the home once again. Many in my family had disdain for Lloyd for a variety of reasons, and several felt his neglect of Genevieve had exacerbated her mental issues. Again, Melvin witnessed this additional violent incident, and the following is what he told me:

> The day he passed we were all sitting outside. Church members were coming around. Lloyd was sitting in a lawn chair in front of the double-paned glass window. Marvin and Stanley pulled up, and they walked up real quiet, just chill. I remember Marvin picking up a lawn chair and slamming it on Lloyd's head, and it shattered the big glass window. Stanley, he was the biggest man, and he walked up and got hold of Lloyd, but Lloyd got loose and started running.
>
> Stanley wasn't running, he was walking beast mode down Oneida toward Lloyd, and Lloyd was running. He ran off and didn't come back. It was such a dramatic part of my life. It was crazy.
>
> We went into the house, and everyone got cold rags to put on Mother's head, trying to keep her calm. The police

THE CRIPPLING OF MY JOY

came, and she said she refused to press charges against
Genevieve for murder. Instead of jail, they put her in a mental institution.

Growing up, our house had been known as a place of peace. All
this chaos baffles me to this day.

I didn't get to Denver until two days later. Heads were calmer
by then.

When I first heard about my dad, I called Dr. Robert H. Wilson
Sr., my pastor in Dallas. Dr. Bob, as he was affectionately called, was
one of the most well-known Black preachers in the country. I told
him my sister had shot Dad and I didn't know how to get home. The
Buick LeSabre I owned at the time was about ten years old and might
not make the trip. The next day he met Lynne and me at the airport
and bought us round-trip tickets to Denver on Braniff Airways. Dr.
Bob said to me, "You've lost your dad, but I'll be your dad now." He
became a very important person in my life.

My mother and one of my sisters greeted us at the airport. I was
not sure what to expect when I went to embrace them, but I recall my
mother being in charge of her emotions.

We wandered around the Oneida Street house in a malaise
because the main source of strength in the family was gone. Mother
became very positive, wanting to pull everyone together, to continue
to have hope and faith, to rely on God. Even in the face of seeing her
husband shot in the forehead a few feet away from her, and despite
almost getting shot herself, she kept saying, "God's going to see us
through this."

I remember a local minister came to the house expecting a somber situation, despair at its highest level. What he found was hope and
laughter. It bothered him. He wanted to have prayer and indicated

that he was troubled we were not downtrodden. But that was not where we were. That was not where our parents lived. Dad was the one that geared us toward the church, but my mother was the heart of the home. She had a solid steel exterior, which she transferred to us. There was limited weeping.

Looking back, I see we were depriving ourselves of raw emotion where we could outwardly hurt and cry and be down. When you don't process emotions thoroughly, you put on a mask. As a young person, I didn't have a lot of room for emotions, which created a barrier to experiencing joy. I have learned when we are out of touch with how we feel and with how others feel, we become disconnected from ourselves and others.

Dad's funeral was a huge event at Zion Baptist Church. Zion, with its handsome historic stone façade, is the oldest Black church in the Rocky Mountains. The pastor at the time was Rev. Dr. Wendell T. Liggins. Dr. Liggins was president of the Western States Baptist Convention, and Dad had been vice president. Rev. L.J. Jordan of Waterloo, Iowa, an evangelist who occasionally preached revivals for our church, rode the eighteen-hour Greyhound bus to come preach Dad's eulogy. There was a community choir led by the minister of music who also taught at Manual High School where Dad worked. Mother and all the women in our family wore black but added color and flowers. They refused to attend as a somber group.

My father was one of the meekest and mildest of individuals, and he provided outstanding ministerial leadership. He was beloved, and his words of wisdom and comfort were often sought by people who found themselves troubled in life. His loss was not just a family death; it was a community injury.

Less than a year after Genevieve shot Dad, only one Williams family member remained in Denver: my sister Patricia. My family had scattered to the far ends of the country, to California, Maryland, and Texas. Genevieve was sentenced to the Colorado State Hospital in Pueblo (now Colorado Mental Health Institute). Patricia and her family remained in Denver while Genevieve was in the hospital. Mother left Denver and simply moved around, visiting each of her children for extended periods. We didn't have very much contact with one another.

We later understood that amid the entanglement of paranoid schizophrenia, Genevieve went to a pawn shop on Colfax Avenue and purchased a .22 caliber revolver.[23] She claimed she heard voices. In one version, she said she heard voices telling her to kill her parents, and in another version, my father's voice was constantly in her head—and she thought killing him was the only way to silence it.

I was not aware of my sister's mental issues until after I had gone away to Bishop College. I understand now my dad had been trying to get her mental help and treatment.

Genevieve was three years ahead of me in school. She married Lloyd before she graduated from high school, and they had a baby. We all had high hopes and expectations for her. She was bright and bubbly and had a terrific personality. I considered her smart, though she did not go to college, and she was a good piano player.

In my freshman year in 1973, when I came home for Christmas, the family started telling me Genevieve was acting peculiar. She had stopped going to my dad's church. She and Lloyd had started going to another church where they had a tradition of casting demons out of people. It was a Christian congregation but very different from the churches to which we were accustomed.

Genevieve and her husband were struggling financially. They often needed a ride, and that duty fell on me when I was still living at home. I was given a car in high school, a blue 1962 Chevy Bel Air station wagon, so I could help people get to church. I went to visit her at work once or maybe to pick her up. She was pregnant and working hard, mopping and cleaning and doing a whole lot of physical labor. I remember wondering where Lloyd was.

Lloyd rarely held a job. In general, Lloyd was nowhere around at work time, but he rarely missed our Sunday dinners. My sister Patricia and I talked about him sponging off Dad. Many felt he wasn't holding up his end of the marriage. Several folks even attribute Genevieve's mental health problems to him. My feeling is he might have hastened her condition by not being a helping hand.

While I was not aware at the time that she had threatened my parents before, she did make threats from the mental institution and later. She had written down stories about wanting to kill all of us. Years later, when her children were grown, they told me they found writings she had taped under a countertop where she spelled out plans to harm members of the family.

After a few years, my sister was deemed fit to reenter the community with no restrictions. She went back to Denver to the church Dad had organized. With my years of training and in social services, it is a big mystery to me how she got her kids back. She got married again to Kenneth Woolbright, a member of Dad's church. Every time I saw Kenneth, he always had on a big smile, but he was slow-speaking and exceptionally timid. It seemed that some people were put off by Kenneth because of his mannerisms, but he loved Dad because my father did not treat him like he was different and because Dad gave him a job cleaning the church after worship. Kenneth thought Dad was one of the greatest people in the world, and marrying Reverend Williams's daughter was the prize of his life. In some ways I often felt Kenneth transferred his lofty thoughts of Dad onto me. To him I was the preacher following in Reverend Williams's footsteps.

Once when I was back in Denver and working in child protective services, Genevieve's kids called me—they were grown by then—and said she was acting bizarre. They wanted me, a social worker, to help them help her. I went to her apartment and suggested she get a mental health evaluation. She stood up and said, "Get the f*** out of my house." This was not the response I expected. Profanity was not part of our upbringing. I sat there for a second until she said it again. Then I left.

I talked to my colleagues in adult protection services about Genevieve. An attorney on staff told me they typically looked for patterns with patients. The pattern with Genevieve was that when Dad was trying to help her as her father and a minister, she killed him. The attorney advised me not to follow that pattern.

We could not escape the fear she created in our family as she, who was not jailed for her crimes, continued to threaten the lives of my family physically and emotionally. As a social worker, I was able to get her admitted to the county hospital on a seventy-two-hour hold, which turned into a longer confinement. Eventually, her daughter got guardianship because my sister was deemed a risk to herself and others.

Today, my sister lives in a secured assisted living facility in Colorado. I visit her every time I go to Denver, annually or every other year. Lynne and I went to see her last in 2019. It is like a nursing home, though she can't leave. Her husband, Kenneth, visits her regularly.

I have not heard anyone say she ever asked for forgiveness. Nevertheless, I immediately forgave Genevieve, all the way back in 1976. It was a learned behavior in my family culture. And I do believe true healing only comes when we forgive. Forgiveness is essential, but forgiving and forgetting are not the same thing.

God asked Cain, "Where is your brother Abel?" after Cain murdered him. Cain responded, "I do not know; am I my brother's keeper?"

(Genesis 4:9). In the Genesis account, this question is not answered. Most Christians answer this question affirmatively. I do not.

Keepers of other people are controllers of other people. That's what prisons do. I am not called to be Genevieve's keeper, but I am called to be her brother. Brothers and sisters have a responsibility to care about and show love to one another. I not only visit her but also have helped her along the way when she needed assistance, such as with rent money. A brother does not want his sister to go homeless.

For decades following my father's murder, part of me sought to understand people like my sister who were driven to commit evil deeds. Many of them ended up in prison, though she did not. I sought in this journey an understanding of mental illness, of how poverty, neglect, and abuse manifest in people. I discovered, in a way, I was in another kind of prison, one created by a set of circumstances in my life: violence, loss, job insecurity, separation from family, and unfulfilled expectations.

For some time after Dad's murder, Dr. Bob and Cornerstone Baptist Church of Christ Jesus in Dallas became my anchors. Of course, Lynne was a constant good in my young adult life too. She and I carried on, yet I had lost my footing. This devastation in my family—my father's death, my sister's instability, my siblings' fleeing—ignited an underlying anxiety that stayed with me for years. I was operating in a daze, apprehensive about what was around the next corner. Like my family after my sister's shameful act, I fell prey to the desire to hide my pain from others. I talked and preached with confidence, but it was a masked performance because I did not want anyone to know I felt defeated.

I will never understand acts of passion and momentary insanity like murder. I must be satisfied with knowing I cannot fathom such violence. What I do know is the love and teachings of Jesus

Christ are a salve for my deep wounds of hopelessness. Dad's murder and continued personal challenges left me feeling disjointed and out of place. Joy was suppressed for me as a young adult. Every human being feels this way at one time or another. I was locked inside a prison I created, unable to grab hold of joy.

Attempts to Connect

When we visited Genevieve in the years that followed, we felt it was somewhat our Christian duty to tell her that she was forgiven by God and by us. This act of forgiveness we demonstrated masked all the pain between us. We did not talk about what happened or why she killed our father. We did not discuss the pain we lived with. Instead, we gathered around a piano in a community room where Genevieve played "Jesus, Keep Me Near the Cross," and we sang to her playing. We all cried as we sang without any conversation about what our tears meant.

Often the unmentioned victims in my dad's murder were Genevieve's three young children: Marvel, age four; Lawrence, age two; and Ivan, age six months. While Genevieve served five years in the Colorado State Hospital, many family members kept Genevieve's children—but they were returned to her after those five years.

Every year I made at least one trip to Denver, and even though I did not have regular contact with Genevieve, I made a trip to her home to see her, her kids, and her new husband. All my other siblings had moved from Denver, and I was her only contact with our family. When I would visit, her family was on various forms of public assistance or disability income for sustenance. Lynne always went with me because she cared, and she did not want something to happen to me. The visits were always brief, and we never discussed what happened that bleak August day in 1976. I wanted her kids to know they had an uncle who wanted to know them, and I would bring her up to date on what I knew about our siblings.

One year while I visited, Genevieve and Kenneth shared that they both had jobs at Denver International Airport working in the department that transported people in wheelchairs. Not only did they have jobs, but they had bought a house and were paying a mortgage. I was happy for my sister and wanted her and her family to have better than they had experienced in the past.

The year after my father's death I dropped out of Bishop College for four years while I worked on various jobs to pay bills. In 1980 I went back to Bishop College for one year, but eventually dropped out again. I thought education was my passport to reach the blessed lands of ministry that I wanted to reside in, but I found myself on the wrong side of education's promised land. I had completed three of the four years needed to graduate and could see the border, but I was miserable because my efforts had fallen short of getting a degree.

Though years passed, the events of 1976 weighed heavily on me. At age thirty-three, I landed a solid job working for the State of Texas, determining the eligibility of public assistance applicants. It was steady work with good pay and benefits, so Lynne and I bought a house in a Dallas suburb. On a financial basis, things were looking up, but I still was not taking any steps toward a ministry that provided for my family. I could see many of my peers from college pastoring churches that supported their families. All that I had dreamed for myself seemed to be happening for everyone else. I was broken inside, but I wore a mask of Christian contentment that did not allow anyone else to know how much internal struggle I endured.

NINE

Late-Night Joy

Nineteen years before I preached a sermon on Death Row about Paul and Silas, I preached on the same scripture in Denver to my congregation at Abundant Life Baptist Church. In preparation for my joy series sermon at Central Prison, I looked back at my notes. I marveled at how far God had brought me from that time. I was like an artist who looks back at their early work and barely recognizes themselves in it.

I, like many, have had midnight hours in my life, times when things looked extremely dark and I could have chosen to—and sometimes did—fall into despair. Losing my father was certainly one of those moments, but there would be plenty more to come: more tragedy within the family Lynne and I had created and hard decisions that led me down to my bleakest points.

Writing prompt for those who are incarcerated:

Midnight symbolically suggests the hour when an individual could easily move from anxiety to dread to despair and, eventually, emotional and

FINDING JOY ON DEATH ROW

spiritual defeat. Midnight is a dangerous hour, and one could easily say, "I give up" in the midnight hour. Paul and Silas are remembered not for their despair but for their expressions of joy. They prayed and sang when it was tempting to give up and give out. They prayed and sang as attempts were made to steal their joy-filled existence. To you, my brothers, locked up here on Death Row: You like all of us can feel that it is the midnight hour. Understand this truth: God made joy for your midnight hour.

The Ideal State of Being

Back on Death Row, five of the six men who attended our small group agreed on my writing prompt about what the "midnight hour" symbolizes—but George Thomas Wilkerson offered pushback. It was not that he completely disagreed. He felt the idea was too restricting to express the larger work God does. George contended that midnight is not the only hour where joy can be experienced. He argued, "I don't think God specifically made joy *for* the midnight hour. Rather, I'm convinced joy is part of the ideal state of being that God is transforming us toward—along with the other fruits of the Spirit, such as peace, patience, etc.; and other qualities, like gratitude, hope, gladness, etc." (see fig. 9.1).

George is the editor of *Compassion*, a bimonthly newsletter written by men and women on Death Row. His leadership in this effort, with help from volunteers outside of prison, enables his abilities with language and logic to reach countless people, those imprisoned and not. You may recall that George was convicted of two first-degree murders and burglary.

George suggested that hope is what gets him through his late-night hours, not joy. People are often inclined to one or the other.

I agree that the "midnight" hour can be an especially trying time of despair, which can lead to defeat both psychologically and spiritually. And I agree that joy can help one get through that dark time. However, I don't think God specifically made joy for the midnight hour. Rather, I'm convinced joy is part of the ideal state of being that God is transforming us toward — along with the other fruits of the Spirit, such as peace, patience, etc.; and other qualities, like gratitude, hope, gladness, etc.

What I mean to say is: God is conforming all believers to the Image of Christ (Rom. 8:28-30), who is His own Image. Joy is the natural, steady state of God and Christ, i.e., their disposition! A lack of joy speaks to our fallen state. No, if there was something that truly seems to help one through a dark hour, it's HOPE — that reasonable confidence that God will accomplish His will. Amen.

STORY

I understand "hope" to mean "the reasonable confidence that something I desire will come to pass." In scripture God tells me He will never leave me nor forsake me; that for "him whose ways are pleasing to God, He will make even his enemies be at peace with him." There was a time years ago, after I first got locked up, when someone on my pod did something so disrespectful that according to prison culture I had to fight him — or even kill him. I prayed desperately because I did not want to do it. The only way I could get out of it without being victimized by the other bullies was if the guy came and apologized. He was not known to have ever apologized to anyone, so I needed a miracle. I said, "Lord, I need you. I want to do your will. I need you to move in that man's heart and make him apologize — and I will forgive him. Please, Lord, otherwise I will be forced to hurt him or be hurt trying."

Sure enough, a few minutes later, the guy came and apologized. I had hoped in God, and He delivered me. No other test since then, has even come close... Amen. By the way, in the 8 years since, I've not heard of or seen that guy apologizing to anyone else, which further confirms the miracle.

Figure 9.1. Response from George Thomas Wilkerson

Sometimes I shy away from joy myself because it is often tied to happiness. Sometimes I shy away from hope because when you've had multiple disappointments, it can be a struggle to expect good things to happen. We often underappreciate the interconnectivity between joy and hope. Hope rests on joy, and joy rests on hope. George helped me realize I cannot make it day-to-day without either one.

He raised worthwhile issues for consideration.

- Is joy larger than circumstances, having no boundaries?
- Do you need a midnight hour for joy to be revealed?
- Is joy in the midnight hour needed to validate joy's overall significance?

I believe the spiritual awareness of joy to be extraneous to occurrences or outcomes. Joy is not dependent on how we think or feel. Joy exists despite how things are going. Joy exists during good days and bad, in happy moments and in sad, when people are kind or harsh.

Joy is firmly grounded as a principle of God's engagement with humanity. God finds a way to convert the emotional currency of despair, grief, hopelessness, and helplessness into the currency of a brighter outlook through joy. Therapist and writer Miriam Greenspan put it this way:

> For those who desperately need a way to feel more hopeful, resilient, and joyful, take heart! The emotions that appear to afflict us can be the vehicles of our liberation from suffering. Experiencing our grief, fear, and despair in a new light, we renew our capacities for gratitude, joy, and faith. We grow in courage and compassion. We approach the world with less fear and more wonder. We have more energy for changing the things that matter.[24]

Joy is used to turn the bitter anguish of midnight experiences into hope for better times to come.

Christian joy has a spiritual origin, yet there are physical manifestations of joy in our bodies. Our participation in joyous activities sustains us. According to neuroscientist Giovanni Frazzetto, "Moments of joy, time spent smiling and laughing and in general in a good mood do have tangible repercussions on our well-being. Their trace can be found in our bodies."[25] Paul and Silas experienced this in a prison dungeon when they prayed and sang at midnight. That low place and their low time was the right time to practice joy.

God Never Gave Up on Me

In September 1995, Archie Billings was indicted for several offenses, including first-degree murder and first-degree rape. He was tried capitally the following May, and the jury found him guilty of several charges, including first-degree murder based on "premeditation and deliberation and under the felony murder rule." The jury recommended the death penalty for the first-degree murder conviction, and Archie Billings was sentenced to death.[26]

If joy is God's work, finding joy during Death Row's midnight hour can be transformative. Archie wrote, "I find joy that I'm locked up not living the lifestyle I was on the streets dying in my sins not having salvation. People say you can't find joy being in prison, but if you put your trust in 'God,' you will find it" (see fig. 9.2). One would think that the desire to be free from bondage would be greater hope for Archie, but finding God and being removed from his prior life led Archie to greater joy.

The circumstances that led Archie to Death Row did not incapacitate joy for Archie. "When I caught my charges," he wrote, "a preacher in jail kept coming each week talking to me. I wasn't trying to hear it. When I got sentenced to death my attorney gave me a Bible. So I feel that 'God,' never gave up on me and was leading me the whole time so that is what brings me joy."

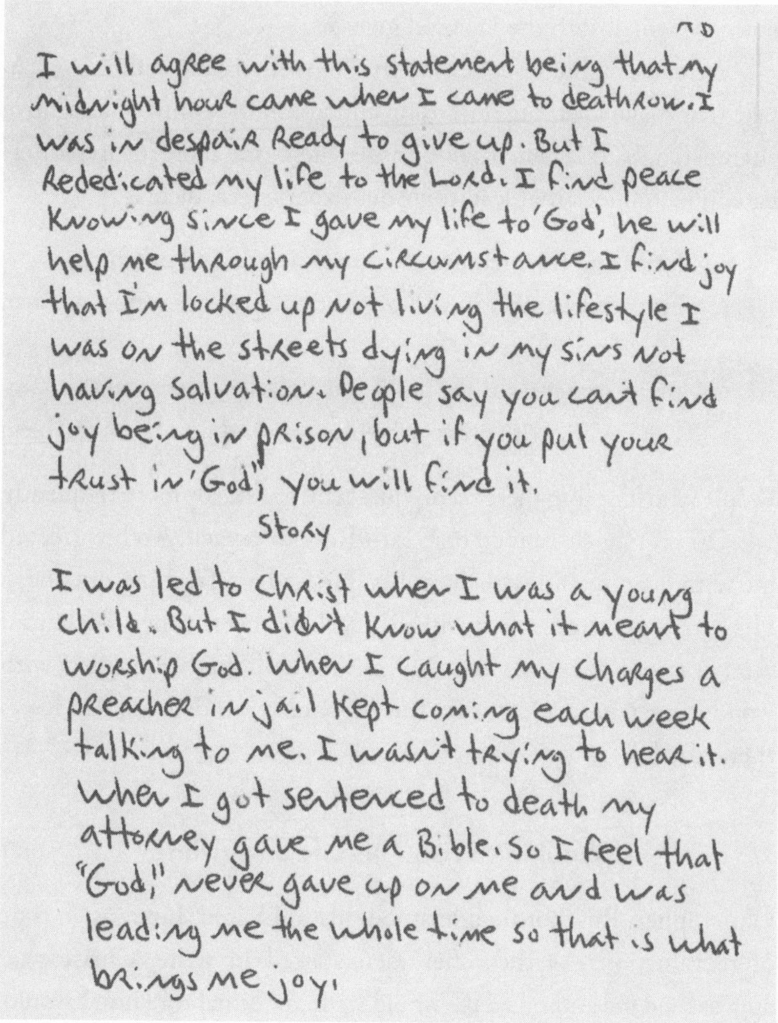

I will agree with this statement being that my midnight hour came when I came to deathrow. I was in despair ready to give up. But I rededicated my life to the Lord. I find peace knowing since I gave my life to 'God', he will help me through my circumstance. I find joy that I'm locked up not living the lifestyle I was on the streets dying in my sins not having salvation. People say you can't find joy being in prison, but if you put your trust in 'God', you will find it.

Story

I was led to Christ when I was a young child. But I didn't know what it meant to worship God. When I caught my charges a preacher in jail kept coming each week talking to me. I wasn't trying to hear it. When I got sentenced to death my attorney gave me a Bible. So I feel that "God," never gave up on me and was leading me the whole time so that is what brings me joy.

Figure 9.2. Response from Archie Billings

Humans are vulnerable to being pulled away from joy and God. Our sinful nature turns us away from God's provisions. Our violations of God's directives cause us harm and cause us to harm our sisters and brothers. The more we align with our fallenness, the less joy we will sense. The more we move away from our fallenness, the more we will absorb the joy God gives us.

We can heighten our sensitivity to joy. There are actions we can take that make joy more rewarding and lessen the control of negative circumstances. It is beneficial to those who desire more joy to participate in techniques that lead to joyous experiences, such as:

- Releasing the pressure to control people and outcomes
- Forgiving anyone whom you hold a grievance against, including yourself
- Being grateful for the good you experience, constantly
- Connecting with others who bless you and whom you can bless

People who lean into these techniques tend to find joy more frequently.

On every visit I made to Death Row to preach, Archie greeted me with a smile and with humility. He had a refreshing openness. His writings lifted my spirits. There have been times I felt that God was not there for me. My midnight hours were filled with wondering where God was. But Archie reminded me God was there all along.

I Wouldn't Wish This Life on Anyone

Christopher Roseboro understood his midnight hour as a time of reevaluation. As the other men started to write, Christopher approached me and asked if I would write for him. I told him I would. He didn't offer a reason he wanted me to write, and I didn't ask. I later learned that Christopher's appeals in court are based on his having an intellectual disability. I specifically remember as Christopher left one of the Sunday worship times, he gave me a fist bump and asked me to pray for him because he had an appeal the next week.

This is my interpretation and paraphrase of what Christopher told me that day:

> In my opinion the statement is true because, at the end of every day, I must think about what I have thought and done. At the end of the day, I see my relationship with God in the midnight hour. At midnight I try to think of how I can better myself for the next day. Knowing I have God is something I can lean on as I try to make it day by day.
>
> Story: In 2005 I felt lonely and a little depressed. I had been thinking about my children, and I had been praying to God that someday I would hear from them. Out of the blue I got a letter from my daughter who was thirteen years old at the time.
>
> I thought I could never connect to another part of me, but every night I would go in my cell and ask God to give me some kind of hope of hearing from my children. When I heard from my daughter a large burden was lifted off my shoulders. In my midnight hour, I knew then that God was with me the whole time, even when I thought that there was no hope.
>
> If we just give God our time, our prayers will be heard. Prayer is the key because it makes a difference when we put our trust in God. At one time I thought God had left me, but I heard that God will never leave us or forsake us. I believe this now because God is real in our lives if we believe.

I can't change everything that is going on, but I can change myself to gain self-respect. This is very hard to deal with when I find myself crying inside because I can't control the crying. One thing I know is that I wouldn't wish this life on anyone. To live on Death Row, you've got to stay away from the negativity. I do that with my Christian brothers who stay positive.

Christopher saw joy as the way to get better, assess what he'd done, and use that as a launching pad for the future. He understood that for the Christian, prayer is an activity that will help to govern and monitor joy. Christopher reported longing to hear from his children, so he prayed to God, and soon thereafter he received a letter from his daughter. He understood that prayer is a stepping-stone to joy.

Christopher called for another step. He advocated for the need to change oneself as a technique in working through the midnight hour. He found a more joyful life by connecting with other men on Death Row who sought the same transformation.

Christopher had been tried for first-degree murder as well as first-degree burglary, first-degree rape, felonious larceny, and possession of stolen property. The jury recommended a sentence of death when he was convicted, and the trial court sentenced him accordingly.[27]

Christopher made me realize that when circumstances are dim, or even dark, I need to stop and assess the moment. Perhaps my extra consideration of events will uncover new pathways to pursue. Christopher indicated his need to stay around his Christian brothers on Death Row to avoid negativity. This is true for me also. I need the fellowship and words that flow from the local church to support me. Without them, I drift toward despair.

I Refuse to Believe He Has Brought Me This Far to Fail Me

Clifford Miller saw God as the overshadowing source of all he needed. When he stopped to look at what God was doing, he found God at the core of the blessing in his life. This evaluation was a part of what moved him to a better spiritual and emotional place.

In October 2001, Clifford Miller was convicted of multiple felonies, including kidnapping and first-degree murder. After finding him guilty of first-degree murder, the jury recommended a sentence of death.[28]

Clifford typically came to Death Row church wired to worship. He frequently volunteered to lead the worship, read the scriptures, or offer a prayer. On Sundays, I could always count on Clifford to help me with the sequence of the worship service. His positivity and

> I BELIEVE THIS TO BE TRUE. WITH SO MANY 'OUTSIDE' INFLUENCES EXPECTING FOR ME TO GIVE UP, I CAN CHOSE TO GO THAT ROUTE. BUT I BELIEVE THAT GOD, WHO IS IN ME, IS STRONGER THAT THESE 'OUTSIDE' VOICES.. PEOPLE WHO EXPECT ME TO FAIL / JUST GIVE UP. BY STAYING FOCUSED ON THE GOD OF THE BIBLE, AND NOT DEPEND ON MY OWN STRENGHT, I BELIEVE HE WILL ALLOW ME TO SEE BETTER DAY'S. I REFUSE TO BELIEVE HE HAS BROUGHT ME THIS FAR TO FAIL ME NOW.

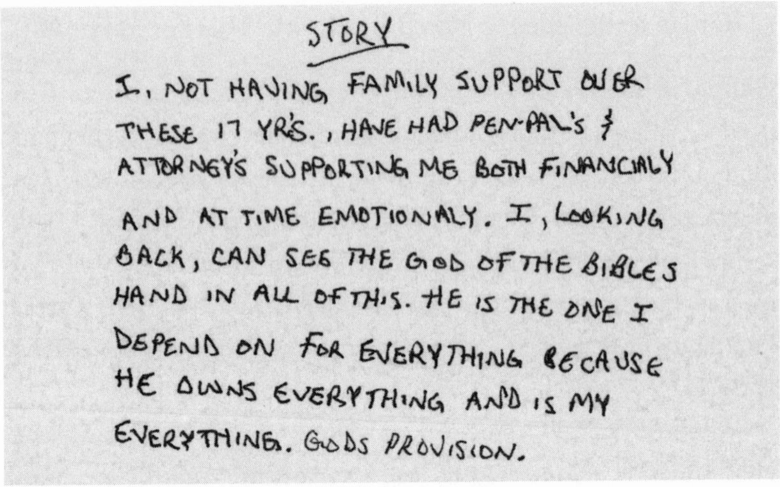

STORY

I, NOT HAVING FAMILY SUPPORT OVER THESE 17 YR'S., HAVE HAD PEN-PAL'S & ATTORNEY'S SUPPORTING ME BOTH FINANCIALY AND AT TIME EMOTIONALY. I, LOOKING BACK, CAN SEE THE GOD OF THE BIBLES HAND IN ALL OF THIS. HE IS THE ONE I DEPEND ON FOR EVERYTHING BECAUSE HE OWNS EVERYTHING AND IS MY EVERYTHING. GODS PROVISION.

Figure 9.3. Response from Clifford Miller

reliance on God appeared in his writings when he said, "I believe [God] will allow me to see better days. I refuse to believe he has brought me this far to fail me now" (see fig. 9.3).

The Whole World in His Hands

Stephen Buckner discussed the midnight hour as to how he coped with the issue of the end of his life and what he expected for life after death. This was gut-wrenching to hear because he had an honesty about dealing with the end of life that each person incarcerated on Death Row must grapple with at some level.

All sober-minded adults realize that at some point every life on earth will come to an end, and we must develop theories about what we expect will happen when our bodies stop functioning. While we know we are going to die, it's difficult to imagine death being pronounced upon us by other humans, that it could be legally acceptable for another person to take our life. Stephen introduced this consideration and the harm he caused his victims and their families. He wrote, "Knowing God is ever present with me, I've this joy, hope of His promise that Heaven awaits me . . . God placed on my heart to ask for forgiveness for the sins I did against them, my victims family members!" (see fig. 9.4). Stephen saw his midnight hour as a time to process his guilt, seek forgiveness and absolution, and build hope in eternal salvation.

Stephen Buckner was charged in January 2008 with three counts of first-degree murder. He was sentenced to death. He also was convicted of one count of attempted first-degree murder and six counts of assault with a deadly weapon.[29] I do not recall any personal conversation with Stephen during my time serving with the men on Death Row. In worship and at the time he came to write, he was quiet and said little. I am glad he took the time to write his thoughts.

> Yes, God has made joy for my midnight hour! I could give up, but I never will for God has placed in me, His Holy Spirit. I remember being locked up five weeks in a cell, isolated from everyone else - but I got a Bible (which brings me joy anytime) and read it out loud for others to hear, in this darkness on another cell block, I and I

Know they others heard too, someone singing "He's got the whole
world in His hands"! when the
officers came by to check on us
I told them about it, and I
started singing too, "He got

the whole World in His Hawds"
too! We brought one soul to
Jesus too — thats JOY-Salvation!

STORY

Knowing God is ever present with
me, I've this joy, hope of His
promise that Heaven awaits me.
But God has given me — something hard that I see; but I
realize my ways are not His
ways, and I Know He'll give
me the strength and words
to use in doing His will. Just
as the story above brought me
joy, I Know God receives the

glory and joy, He has put for me too do-for His will. God placed on my heart to ask for forgiveness for the sins I did against them, my victims family members.

Figure 9.4. Response from Stephen Buckner

"When That Cell Door Close During That Midnight Hour"

Perhaps the most poignant response to the sermon statement came from William Eugene Robinson. He wrote what may be the closest understanding about what happens in their actual midnight hour: "When that cell door close during that midnight hour, it's just me and God." Late at night when all the concerns and distractions of Death Row are shut out and there are no correctional officers, prison staff, or other men, William turns to God.

When I met William, I noticed he was taller than most of the men on Death Row. He also appeared younger. His hair was braided or in twists. William was convicted in 2006 of first-degree murder and first-degree attempted murder in the robbery of a store.[30] He must have presented as a child at the age of twenty-three when he first came to Death Row. He would have just been learning what it meant to give and receive assistance from others as an adult.

William briefly described his daily journey back and forth from his chronological midnight hour to his spiritual midnight hour. You can imagine it through his powerful description: "Every time I leave outside my cell I have to put on that Armor to guard myself from the

That would be so true, fer
the simple fact my reallity
is that I am sentenced to Death,
and threw the day I have
my thoughts from every one, and
thing around me to keep me
going but when that cell
door close ~~and theirs no~~
during that midnight hour, Its
Just me and God. Basiclly
I'm more lost without God in
the light of the day than I
am in the midnight hour.

Story

(When the door (close)

Every night when that Door
close for lock down, ~~●~~ ~~●~~ And
I'm in that cell alone, it
feel like a big weight just
fell off my shoulders, because
every time I leave out side my cell
I have to put on that Armor to

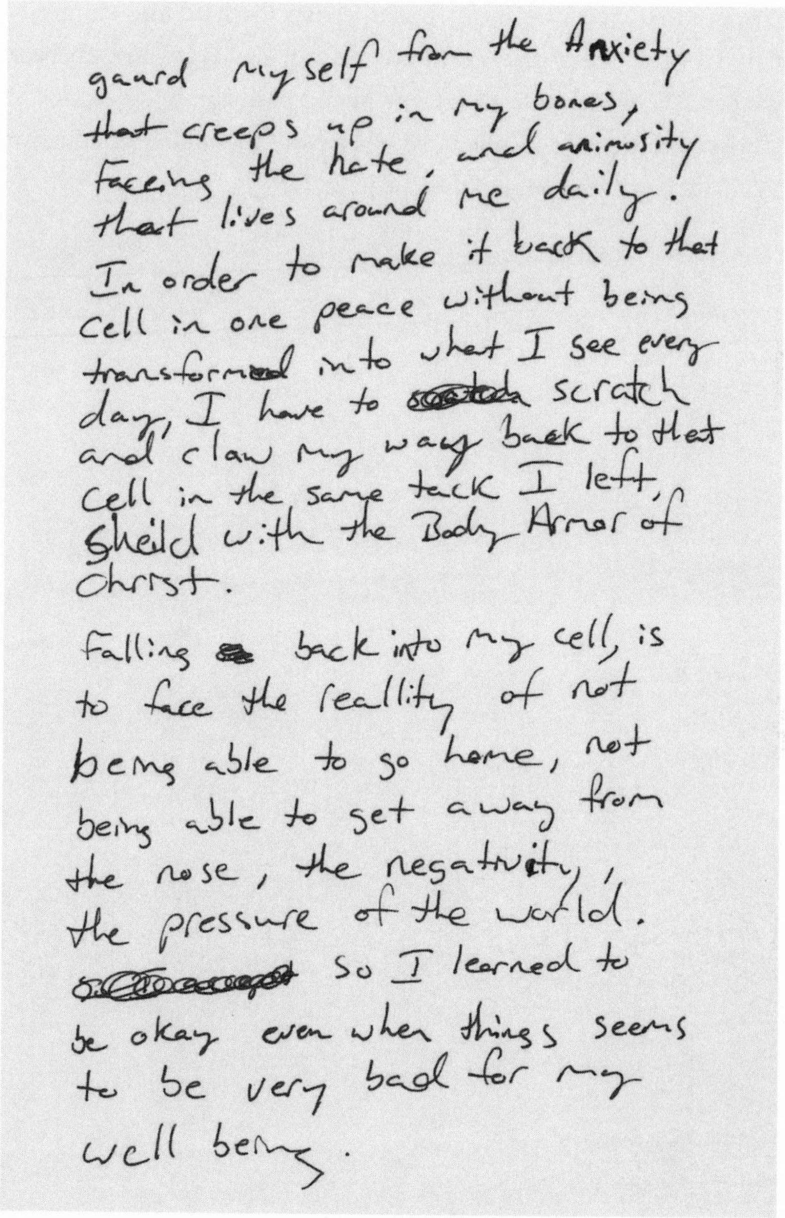

gaurd myself from the Anxiety that creeps up in my bones, faceing the hate, and animosity that lives around me daily. In order to make it back to that cell in one peace without being transformed into what I see every day, I have to scratch and claw my way back to that cell in the same tack I left, sheild with the Body Armor of Chrrst.

Falling back into my cell, is to face the reallity of not being able to go home, not being able to get away from the nose, the negativity, the pressure of the world. So I learned to be okay even when things seems to be very bad for my well being.

Figure 9.5. Response from William Eugene Robinson

Anxiety that creeps up in my bones, facing the hate, and animosity that lives around me daily . . . I have to scratch and claw my way back to that cell in the same tack I left, sheild with the Body Armor of Christ" (see fig. 9.5). While most of us avoid the midnight hour, for William, it is a place of comfort.

TEN

Joy with Shortages

Even when I have plenty, I struggle with shortages. I want more, or the plenty I have creates new desire. What would it be like to have so much money that I never had to worry about spending? To have so much knowledge flowing from my lips, the stroke of my pen, or the tap of my fingers that people wanted to know my thoughts? To have the kind of talent that enthralls masses? To have so much time my stress over obligations and appointments disappeared?

When I discussed this dilemma with the men on Death Row, we reviewed the Gospel of John where Jesus turned water into wine at a wedding in Cana of Galilee. One of my points was that we, like the wedding party of old, often run out of things we want as the wedding hosts ran out of wine for their guests. This struggle is universal. The real lesson is in how we face our shortages and with what support.

Early in my career, I wanted church folk to witness God at work in my life and for them to link what I offered to their personal spiritual development. These desires were fool's gold, and they left me unsatisfied. The stories of shortages on Death Row struck me like a snowball to the face. Most men and the women hung on every word I said. They saw God at work in what I was doing with them and wanted more every time I showed up.

In our Bible story, the wedding hosts were ashamed to be lacking. They wanted their guests to have wine for the festive occasion, but it ran out. To Jesus, the Creator of all, it was an opportunity for new revelation, a miracle. For the men on Death Row, their shortages are likewise a place where God can intervene.

My discussion with the men was about how lack has the potential to create emotional, psychological, spiritual, social, and even physical maladies, especially when our shortages are called out by our peers or enemies. This idea drew more written responses than any other.

It is important to note how individuals will react differently when faced with lack. When someone who has had twenty-twenty vision begins to lose that advantage, it's devastating. Financial shortages are more deeply felt by those accustomed to an abundance of money. Sendhil Mullainathan, a professor at the University of Chicago Booth School of Business, and Eldar Shafir, a professor of psychology and public affairs at Princeton University, identified scarcity when they wrote, "In the real world, the poor and the rich differ in so many ways. Their diverse backgrounds and experiences lead them to have different personalities, abilities, health, education, and preferences. Those who find themselves working at the last minute under deadline may simply be different people."[31]

Self-worth is formulated in childhood from voices of authority. Healthy self-worth derives from feeling good about who you are and how you fit into the world. It is also about accepting imperfections and recognizing your strengths. All of what is needed to have healthy self-worth can germinate in childhood, and a child whose mind is filled with negative self-image can formulate poor self-worth.

The confinement of the men and women to Death Row, and the threat of their impending punishment, multiplies the impact of their often-experienced shortages and their vulnerabilities.

Keep Up the Good Work

Words validating my worth or contributions were rare in my early years. As a young preacher, I served under one of the nation's top preachers, Dr. Robert H. Wilson Sr. He did not believe a preacher should be influenced by compliments about their sermons, so he rarely offered open flattery. Furthermore, he diminished any flattery given. Typically, after I preached, he would say—aloud for everyone to hear from the pulpit—either "Good job, Son" or nothing. If he said nothing, that meant I should have worked on my sermon more.

One Sunday I preached what I perceived to be the most creative sermon of my life, titled "An Environmental Report." Many congregants told me the message was a blessing, but Dr. Bob did not say anything. As I prepared to leave the church that evening, I stopped by his office to get my coat. He said, "Son, we heard real preaching tonight. Keep up the good work." Those words stamped a much-needed endorsement on my ministry. His affirmation lifted me to do better with each sermon I preached in the future. I, like everyone, need to hear that I did good and that I am good.

Writing prompt for those who are incarcerated:

When you don't have what you want, you are vulnerable to ideas and words that draw you toward despair. You will start to speak unkindly to yourself, saying you are inadequate or inferior, that you are by birth or upbringing less of a person than what is needed. Worse yet is to hear that from someone else.

Trusting in Christ Has Relieved Me of Those Burdens

Several men had their self-images damaged in childhood, but not all the responders agreed about shortages. To Clifford Miller and Keith East, vulnerability to shortages was either eliminated or decreased with a strong connection to God through Jesus Christ.

Clifford Miller entered the room with a wide grin and extended his hand toward me for a fist bump. The look on his face suggested he was eager to know the topic for that day's discussion. Keith East, on the other hand, did not get too hyped about things.

Clifford described how inclinations to despair are a spiritual battle where God can keep you away from the negativity of shortages. He wrote, "I am who I am. I don't have 'cus the Father did not give it to me. If He wanted me to have, I'd have . . . I have learned to go to Him for everything, and He has provided" (see fig. 10.1).

Keith East concurred with Clifford. "It depends on who and what a person believes in and their background. If they have a strong foundation in the home or church they will react differently from someone who does not have believe in Christ" (see fig. 10.2).

As mentioned earlier, Miller was convicted of robbery, kidnapping, and murder. Keith East was indicted in August 1994 for two first-degree murders. The jury found him guilty of beating to death a college president and his wife, East's aunt, during a rampage at their vacation home. He was also charged with robbery, larceny, and more. The jury recommended the death penalty for each of the murders.[32]

These two men had dark sides to their life stories, but a flickering of light from God was evident. That flickering was joy at work in their lives.

At the time I was receiving the writings from the men on Death Row, I was concurrently being considered as a candidate to pastor at

Mount Bright Missionary Baptist Church. It had been nearly a year since I had been a candidate at any church. I wanted to pastor, but after dozens of times being passed over, I was vulnerable to the idea that I would miss another opportunity.

NO, I DON'T FEEL NOR THINK THIS
TO BE TRUE. WHY DO I VIEW IT
THIS WAY? BECAUSE I AM WHO I
AM. I DON'T HAVE 'CUS THE FATHER
DIDNOT GIVE IT TO ME. IF HE WANTED
ME TO HAVE, I'D HAVE.
    TO BE VULNERABLE AND INADEQUATE
MEANS TO ME: VULNERABLE IS WEAK,
PREY, VICTIM. INADEQUATE IS UNABLE,
NOT READY, ILL PREPARED.
    BEFORE TRULY LEANING ON CHRIST, I
WAS THOSE. I HAVE LEARNED TO GO TO HIM
FOR EVERYTHING, AND HE HAS PROVIDED.

STORY

BEFORE COMING TO CHRIST, I FELT THAT
I HAD TO LIVE UP TO THE "WORLDS STANDARD.
TO BE A "MANS MAN". I HAD TO LEARN TO
FIGHT OR BECOME A VICTIM IN THE C.Y.A. (OR
CALIFORNIA YOUTH AUTHORITY). I, OVER
THESE 17 YRS, HAVE LEARNED THAT I
DON'T HAVE TO LIVE LIKE THAT. TRUSTING
IN CHRIST HAS RELIEVED ME OF
THOSE BURDENS.

Figure 10.1. Response from Clifford Miller

I wore my low self-worth like you wear a coat on cold days. Clifford's writings reminded me to lean on Jesus as I went to meet with the church leaders. Keith's writings informed me that my belief systems would defend against the despair I felt at the time. As I presented myself to Mount Bright, I pulled off the coat of despair and put on the coat of joy that I had received from the men on Death Row. These men gave me the confidence to tamp down my feelings of falling short.

Clifford also wrote about how being in prison for seventeen years and finding God pulled him away from the vulnerability and inadequacy he experienced as a youth in the California Youth Authority, a former division of the California Department of Corrections. Clifford's words prompted me to reflect on how I resist vulnerability. I have a history of presenting myself as good, wholesome, and ready when sometimes I am bad, incomplete, and unprepared. It is better to be honest about my shortcomings than to deny them to myself and others. To be honest is to recognize our dependence on God.

Keith wrote about his high school singing days when he went to a University of North Carolina event. There, he discovered other gifted singers who made him question his status. Like Keith, I find myself swirling down the drain of comparisons. It took me some time to realize my worth is in my effectiveness to lift my Creator. If I lift myself instead of lifting God, what I do will be distasteful to both God and the people of God. I surrender my abilities to God as I reach people with God message.

Unwanted, Unloved, and Inadequate

What happens when damaging words come from a loved one in your home or from a parent who is supposed to be an uplifter? Such

yes and NO,' It depends on who
And what a person beleives in
And their Background, If they
Have a strong foundation in the
Home or church they will
React differently From some one
who does not have Beleive
in christ.

your Belief system Will Help you react to
despair, in christ I was taught He will
listen and guide you It took me a long
time to learn the Answer to All lifes
Problems can Be found in the Bible
these are the things my family Had
Been telling me for 35 years But
I Have only come to understand in
the last 15 years Here on the ROW

STORY

There was a time in my life when
I was the Golden child much was
expected. But as I grew older I found
out there were others Just like me.
I Remember the time I was All set
to Attend Voice camp At UNC 16 years old
2 weeks Nothing But singing H.S. Kids

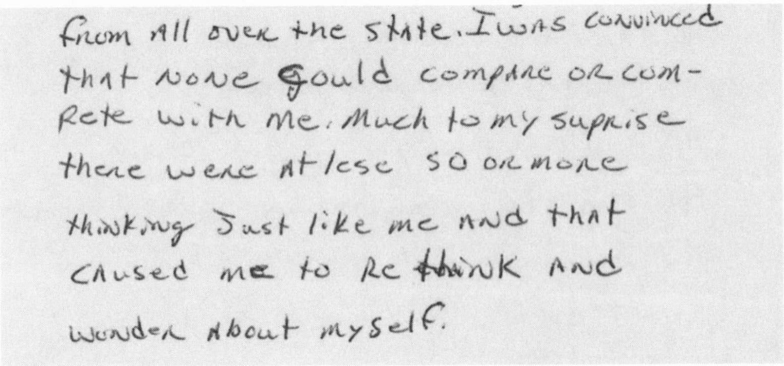
from All over the state. I was convinced
that none could compare or com-
pete with me. Much to my suprise
there were at lese 50 or more
thinking Just like me and that
caused me to re think and
wonder about myself.

Figure 10.2. Response from Keith East

was the case with Mario Phillips. Damaging words from his abusive grandmother impacted him (see fig. 10.3).

I have a fond memory of Mario. On one visit, I told the men they all had at least one more chance at forgiveness. I asked them to put up their index finger to indicate their one more chance. Following that message—and every time I saw Mario thereafter—he said nothing. He would just put up his index finger.

In December 2003, Mario Phillips was indicted for four counts of first-degree murder. He was also indicted for attempted murder, aggravated first-degree kidnapping, arson, and more. In October 2007, a jury found Mario guilty of all four murder counts, attempted first-degree murder, and several other counts. The jury recommended a sentence of death for each murder conviction after a capital sentencing hearing.[33]

Tall, lanky Mario wore a smile suggesting a happy-go-lucky approach to life. After learning of his childhood torments, I wondered if his jovial presentation was a façade masking his pain.

Mario reminded me of my younger self when I sought to be witty despite being unhappy about my life. I didn't think it manly to

its not neccessary true to
how I will, would feel about
hearing that from somebody, however
yes it would, have an impact
on Me only if I believe it
to be true in its entirety,

and from experiences in my
life, there are and has been
times, where I tend to allow
others words, or false statements
about Me, or words directed
at Me to take affect and
I would process it as if
it was true, when it wasn't
only because I was
Vunerable. and ~~an~~ unsure
of Myself, and the direction
my life ~~and~~ ~~the directi~~ is
going in.
Being Vunerable. to Me is
being unsure of myself and
therefore. exposing myself to
all my weaknesses, and allowing
myself, to be accessible to

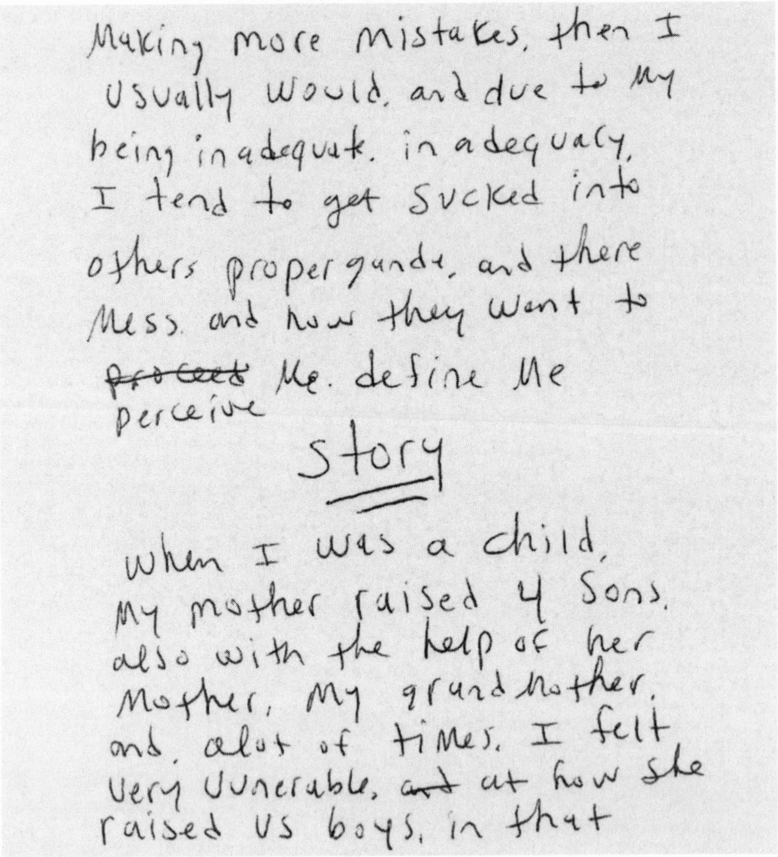

Making more mistakes, then I
usually would, and due to my
being inadequate. inadequacy,
I tend to ~~get~~ sucked into
others proper gande, and there
mess. and how ~~they~~ went to
~~protect~~ Me. define Me
perceive

Story

when I was a child,
my mother raised 4 sons.
also with the help of her
Mother, my grandmother.
and, alot of times. I felt
very vulnerable, ~~and~~ at how she
raised us boys, in that

Figure 10.3. Response from Mario Phillips

be dejected. I didn't think it spiritual to be depressed. So I covered my angst with a smile or humor. People assumed I was happy, but truly I was just unrecognizable. Like myself, maybe Mario was trying to feel good about himself by making others smile, even if it was a cover-up.

Mario's conclusion about finding something about himself that he liked refreshed my soul, as we all need to make the effort to find something about ourselves that we like.

In the years since I met Mario, he has been working to reconcile with his family. Recently, as an addendum to his earlier writings, he wrote the following regarding his mother:

> My momma tried so hard to shelter her four boys from the evil in the world as much as she could. All her best efforts and attempts to do her best to protect us she failed . . . After our father abandoned us, mom and his four sons, to start another family while already having a family. Therefore us four brothers didn't have the luxury of being children, kids anymore, but had to learn to become men fast . . . or else we wouldn't been able to remain as a family . . . Because there was no father figure in my life I started to act out eventually, smoking, drinking, having sex with girls my age and older than, and at school getting into fights a lot and suspended a lot and caught stealing . . . Mom didn't know what to do with me. I started getting into juvenile trouble with the law. So mom started discipline me . . . Mom loved me as much as any parent could love there child. It wasn't her fault, but my own, getting into trouble with the law. I felt so lost, confused, and burdensome. Mom, being young herself, needed a break from us boys and all the stress and pressure of raising four sons alone. So Mom would take us to live with her mother, our grandmother, for periods. There I felt unloved at times because Mom would leave us there, [and] I would really miss her.

Always Thankful

In June 1991 twenty-year-old Nathan Bowie and an uncle were charged with the murders of two men they believed had shot another relative. Nathan believed he was firing in defense. Nathan shared his belief that the two men were armed in an interview posted as a YouTube video created by the North Carolina Coalition for Alternatives to the Death Penalty. Additionally, there is significant evidence that his court-appointed defense attorney was an alcoholic and was under the influence when representing Nathan's case.[34] In February 1993, Nathan was sentenced to death.

Nathan admits he did wrong in taking someone's life. But he also believed he would get a fair trial with competent legal representation. This case highlights how those on Death Row often have less than adequate legal counsel. According to the Innocence Project, as of January 2020, the organization had "documented over 375 DNA exonerations in the United States. Twenty-one of these exonerees had previously been sentenced to death. The vast majority (97%) of these people were wrongfully convicted of committing sexual assault and/or murder."[35]

It is also a great irony that many who end up on Death Row cannot afford—and are not afforded—strong legal counsel, while at the same time, the financial costs associated with death penalty cases are higher than life sentences without parole. According to the Death Penalty Information Center:

> The death penalty is far more expensive than a system utilizing life-without-parole sentences as an alternative punishment. Some of the reasons for the high cost of the death penalty are the longer trials and appeals required when a person's life is on the line, the need for more lawyers and experts on both sides of the case, and the relative rarity of executions.[36]

In short, because the death penalty is a government program fraught with legal expenses, the taxpayer's burden is greater. One must wonder how different outcomes would be if those tax dollars were instead spent on stronger legal defenses for the accused.

But back to Nathan Bowie. It is reported that between an abusive home life and years in an abusive orphanage environment, Nathan did not grow up in safety. On top of physical abuse, words often are

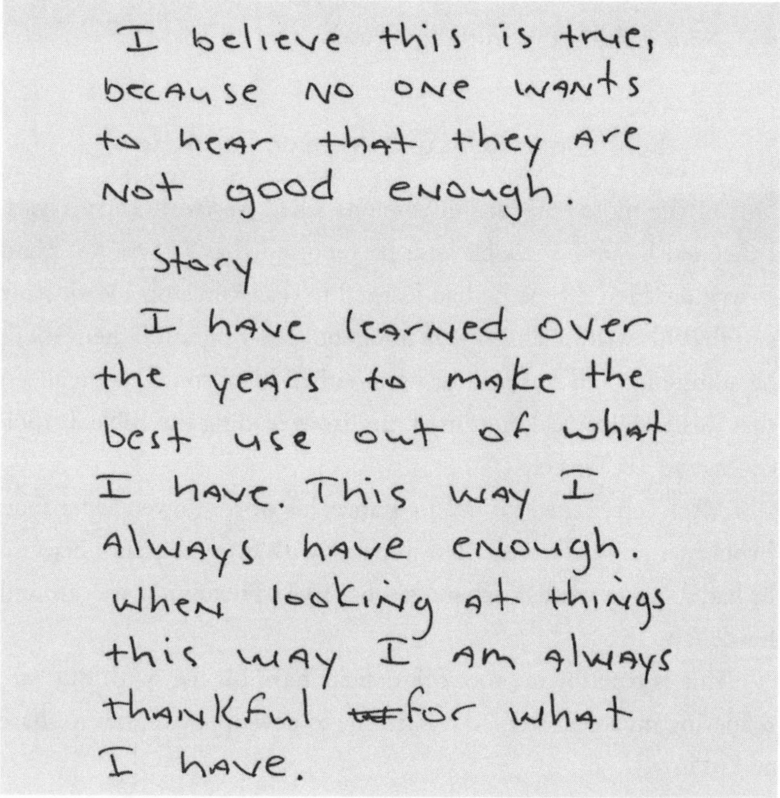

> I believe this is true, because no one wants to hear that they are not good enough.
>
>   Story
>   I have learned over the years to make the best use out of what I have. This way I always have enough. When looking at things this way I am always thankful ~~too~~ for what I have.

Figure 10.4. Response from Nathan Bowie

verbal sticks and stones that break the psyche and cause injury to a person's spirit. Still, Nathan wrote, "I have learned over the years to make the best use out of what I have. This way I always have enough" (see fig. 10.4).

Nathan's positive attitude from within Death Row endorsed my credo to make the best with what you have. Like a card player must learn to play the best they can with the cards they are dealt, I have had to apply this idea to my life. Sometimes you don't get the "good" cards, but you can decide to play a competitive game and maybe even win. Nathan drove this truth home for me.

Learning to Read and Write on Death Row

One of the most poignant discussions I had was with Terry Hyatt. I dictated his responses because he reported that he was not good at writing. He told me he had learned to read while on Death Row and that his writing ability was not good. Terry's grandfather, whom he admired, could not read or write either. In prison, Terry realized that this inability had prevented him from reading the Bible. It took courage to ask for help.

After Terry asked for my assistance, his words flowed faster than I could write. I had to ask him to pause with every sentence because he had so many words to share (see fig. 10.5). He found a way around his deficit.

This is true for me too. My deficits have hit me hard. But surrendering my losses to God has led me to new opportunities to share and to love.

At the time Terry opened up to me, I knew I had to do the same as I presented myself as a pastoral candidate at Mount Bright. Some on their search committee were looking for a whooping preacher in the Black Church tradition, of which I was not. I promised I would work diligently to provide a solid and thought-provoking message in every sermon. That truthfulness seemed to connect with them. My time with Terry helped me when I needed it most.

Vulnerability is a fact in my life, because of my own ignorance. I adopted the idea that it was alright to not learn to read and write and little did I know at the time that I was not opening a door to a brand new world. For years I kept it shut, just like I did with the Lord. Now that I have opened those doors they have both opened up a brand new life. The world sees vulnerability as a crutch, but after coming to know the Lord vulnerability is a great prize to strive for with the Lord. It means you are dependent on Him.

Story

My grandfather, whom I looked
up to, could not read and write
and I thought it was ok. All
you needed was a trade. You
did not need to know how to
read or write. As I grew
older I learned I was
crippling myself, which made
me real vulnerable to grab
hold of any thing, but now
that I have come to know
the Lord and have learned to
read I realize it is one of
the great blessings and tools
that He allows me to us to
get to know Him better. It
sure don't mean that I'm
perfect now or ever can be in

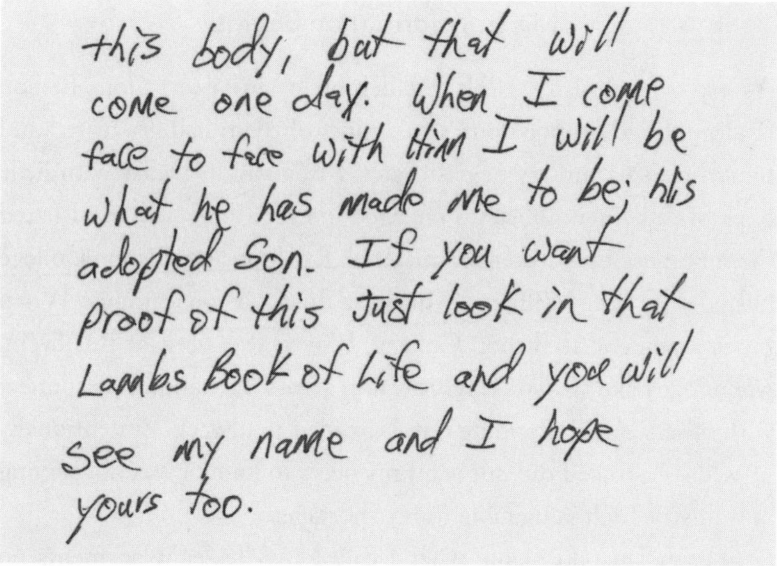
this body, but that will
come one day. When I come
face to face with Him I will be
what he has made me to be; his
adopted Son. If you want
proof of this just look in that
Lambs Book of Life and you will
see my name and I hope
yours too.

Figure 10.5. Response from Terry Alvin Hyatt, transcribed by Dewey Williams

Terry Alvin Hyatt was indicted in May 1999 for two counts of kidnapping, robbery, rape, and first-degree murder charges, all of which related to events that took place in 1979. He was tried capitally in Buncombe County in January 2000. The jury returned guilty verdicts for each charge, and he was sentenced to death for both murder verdicts. Additionally, the trial court sentenced Terry to six consecutive terms of life imprisonment for other convictions.[37]

Terry's words revealed superior spiritual wisdom. For a man who did not learn to read until he was on Death Row, Terry taught me, a pastor with a master of divinity degree from a prestigious university, a spiritual lesson. His sincerity and desire to share his story moved me and humbled me too.

My Transformation Begins

As a young minister, I felt left behind by my peers from Bishop College. I had dropped out, while most of them had graduated and moved on to seminary or pastorates. I was still in Dallas with little hope of full-time ministry. I engaged in every job I had, but I hated them because they weren't ministerial. Every spring, Bishop College hosted the L.K. Williams Ministers' Institute on campus. When I was a student at Bishop College, I loved the week of this event, when many alumni would return from across the nation to reconnect with others. After dropping out, I dreaded that week. I intentionally missed it because I did not want my peers to know I was not serving in ministry. I felt vulnerable to my shortages.

Often I would blame what I called my "lesser" placements on my nature and my nurture. During seasons of despair, I found myself thinking I didn't have the gifts others had or the upbringing, education, or mentoring opportunities. I thought if I were a more talented person, I'd be where my peers were. This pondering neglected God.

God made me who I am and placed all I need around me. My transformation began when I started liking myself, liking what God had put in me, and liking how God had chosen to use me. As I grew into being an instrument of God, I began to see more and more of the good God had done and is doing in me—shortages and all.

ELEVEN

Joy Grows Dim

During my young adult years, I also lost my mother. My father was my motivation, but my mother was my compass for what was right and good in life. I had spent countless hours watching how she managed life and listening to how she handled people as a Christian woman. My mother was not a formally educated person. I believe she only went to the eighth grade, but she produced the church bulletin every Sunday for our church and sent out letters for my dad and the church when needed. She was an excellent Bible teacher who brought passion to her teaching.

If you recall, my mother and two of her grandchildren were in the car when my sister shot and killed my father. None of them ever went to counseling after witnessing this traumatic incident. After my father's death, my mother started traveling around the nation visiting relatives. For much of the next six years, she saw my siblings and their children who lived in Des Moines, Baltimore, Louisiana, and California. She would spend months with them, being a blessing wherever she was. I suspect that her travels were an escape from the pain of losing the man she loved at the hand of her daughter. Perhaps the trauma of the violent end to his life pushed her to find other places to spend time.

In 1982 Lynne was sick, and my mother dropped everything and came to Dallas to help me with our two young daughters. She stayed with us for six weeks. What a gift she was. She cooked and cleaned and did the little girls' hair, a task I never could do well. She slept in the living room on our sofa and helped us with the day-to-day tasks, but she also was a boon to my faith while she visited.

When she was there, our finances were shaky, and many things were lacking, but Mother always made a point to encourage our faith toward trusting God. On one occasion, she was riding with me in my old 1974 Chrysler Sebring. I kept having to put oil in it, and everywhere I drove it, it left a smoke trail like an air force jetliner going across the skies. While on a Dallas freeway, I complained that I needed a better car but could not afford to get one. My mother redirected my thought patterns when she said, "Boy, look at all these thousands of cars in Dallas. Don't you think God can help you get one?" My mother helped me with faith against my dejection and defeated mindset.

One Friday evening in October 1982, she received a phone call indicating that Genevieve, my sister, was resuming old mental health patterns. This call must have reminded her of the horrific day her husband, my father, died. It was as if my mother had a flashback; she grew saddened and fearful. I did not know what post-traumatic stress disorder was at the time, but she must have gone quickly into the grips of this disorder. Mother lay down on our sofa that night, and she never woke up again. On Saturday, paramedics took her to the hospital by ambulance, and on Sunday morning, she was pronounced dead from congestive heart failure and kidney failure. It was as though her body shut down.

Suddenly, both my father and mother were gone. I attempted to be stoic, and I presented myself as the strong soldier of Christian ministry who kept his hand to the gospel plow. I was projecting that I was the one who displayed strength, not giving myself room for sorrow, anger, or feelings of loss. My mother died, and my task was to wear a mask of conquering through the trials of the moment.

A Hard Road Grows Harder

Ten years later, Lynne's mother started having health problems in Denver, and Lynne was making trips from Dallas to see about her monthly. We had a bittersweet existence in Dallas, and the bitter seemed to be more dominant than the sweet. For me, the lack of ministry opportunities was the most heartbreaking, and for Lynne, the consistent financial troubles were the most painful. We decided to move to Denver, where we grew up and where Lynne's mother and family lived. The only one from my family left in Denver was Genevieve.

My experience determining eligibility for public assistance in Texas landed me a job with Boulder County Social Services doing the same work. Then one day my life changed. I was opening mail at my desk when I came across a letter from the Colorado Department of Human Services saying the state had settled a lawsuit. They had been charged with not hiring enough minority child-protection workers and, as a result, were making funds available to pay for education toward a bachelor's or master's degree in social work. The only caveat was that you had to work two years for one of the counties as a child-protection caseworker once you graduated.

A new degree program offered a bachelor of science in social work at Metropolitan State College of Denver. I was accepted to start in August 1996. I finished this degree program in May of 1998.

Though I was living in Denver, I was working in Boulder. So I decided to apply to switch to Denver Human Services to avoid spending an hour going to and from work. My experience landed me a job as a lead eligibility specialist in Denver.

While all this change was happening, a friend, Raymond Groves, called me and asked me if I were interested in pastoring a church. He knew a church looking for a pastor, so he connected me with the Abundant Life Baptist Church leaders in the Montbello community of Denver. They informed me that they were small and could not offer a preacher a large salary. I didn't care, because I had twenty years of sermons bottled up in me that I wanted to release. After an interview and one opportunity to preach, I was hired as the second pastor of a young congregation in September of the same year I started back to school.

Suddenly in August and September 1996, I was pastoring a church as a full-time student and a full-time employee. I was as busy as a bee trying to produce some sweet honey for the Word. I was not studying ministry in school, but I thought it might lead me back to connecting as a minister. I received a raise as a lead worker, so my income was better than before. And I was getting to preach—which was what gave me the most joy.

Lynne was doing customer service for the Yellow Pages in Colorado, so she also had a good income. We were able to help our oldest daughter, Charity, attend Paine College in Augusta, Georgia. Tiffany, our youngest daughter, received a full-ride scholarship to North Carolina A&T State University, plus other academic scholarships provided her beyond what her school cost.

From 1996 to 1998 our schedule was filled up, but it was good. One Sunday night, I received a phone call from Otis Moss III, pastor of the Tabernacle Baptist Church in Augusta. I had known him from when he was youth minister at the New Hope Baptist Church in Denver. He and his wife, Monica, had been treating our oldest daughter, Charity, to Sunday dinner after church when Charity had a seizure and slumped over, passing out at the dinner table. In short order, Lynne and I found ourselves headed to Augusta to bring Charity home as the school had indicated she had a seizure on campus.

One of the saddest days of my life was this trip back to Denver. We loaded Charity's possessions in a rented vehicle and started toward home. As night fell, we decided to stop at a motel in Mississippi to spend the night. Charity was in the bathroom getting ready to take a shower when Lynne and I heard her collapse in the bathroom. We had never seen her have a seizure before. We lifted her from the floor onto the motel bed. Once she was resting there, Lynne collapsed in my arms, crying, "What's wrong with my baby? What's wrong with my baby?" as she pounded her fist into my chest.

These were petit mal seizures. We had read up about these seizures and learned it was best not to call for an ambulance because most people who do that end up with large bills for medical services but no remedies or answers. These seizures caused brief, sudden lapses of consciousness where Charity would not be aware of herself, where she was, or what she was doing. If she were standing, she would fall. If she were sitting, she would fall over in her seat. After about ten minutes, Charity would regain consciousness with no recollection of the seizure.

Charity's illness changed my life and Lynne's, turning us upside down. We went from being a couple in our early forties with an empty nest to having an adult daughter living with us. Charity tried to work, but within a few days, she would have a seizure on the job;

and since she was on a probationary period, they would let her go. Lynne and I spent every dollar we had trying to find out what was causing Charity's seizures. We took her to doctors for six years. We tried medical treatments, holistic treatments, and even brain surgery that hospitalized her for twenty days. We finally filed for bankruptcy because the expenses kept mounting.

TWELVE

Joy in Community

Most sermons about when Jesus turned water into wine at a wedding in Cana of Galilee deal with the miracle. Jesus transformed the most common liquid available on earth into one of life's most desired beverages. He took something easily accessible and, in the presence of the community and dignitaries, made it into that which requires time and preparation to obtain.

It's easy to understand the sermonic draw of a message about God taking that which is common and making it into that which is precious, and in a spectacular way. A second common theme that preachers and teachers discuss in this text is how obedience will lead to blessings in life. Bible preachers and teachers use these verses to prod followers into becoming obedient disciples to Jesus Christ in the hope that Jesus will perform similar miracles in their lives. I wonder how many times this heavy-handed pitch has been proclaimed to congregants.

I was able to share my sermon about Jesus's miracle with both the men and the women of Death Row on separate occasions. When I preached my sermons to the men it was in auditorium-style seating, and I was behind a lectern, but when the sermon was presented to the women, we sat around tables and alternated reading. In both sessions, I stressed how Jesus utilized His disciples to bring about the miracle and how Jesus's disciples could be an essential part of their journey on Death Row. God has created us with a need for one another, so we are designed with interdependence. I encouraged them to be brothers and sisters in Christ and to help one another in their daily lives.

One of my favorite authors, Christian psychologist Larry Crabb, gave an account of how a Sunday school class came together to aid and support his wife, Rachael, when her father died:

> We also have the means to stimulate each other to love and good deeds, to identify, nourish, and help release the good urges that are always there beneath the bad. Connecting among Christians helps to vivify our spirits . . .
>
> Whatever else was happening in their hearts that evening, perhaps ugly things like jealousy . . . or self-pity . . . the overwhelming sense was that better things ruled in our community as we related. People found what was good within them in the middle of whatever was bad, and they released it.[38]

Death Row can be a lonely place. Penal systems remove convicted criminals from free communities by design. Time in prison is for contemplating errors and promoting a desire to avoid them following release (penance). On Death Row, the feelings of isolation and solitude are intensified as the men and women have little if any contact with the outside community and no contact with others in General Population. Seclusion permeates the culture of Death Row.

Three men who reflected on this sermon unanimously agreed about the need for support from the other Christian men on Death Row.

Writing prompt for those who are incarcerated:

When shortages occur in your life, you need the Savior; but you also should
not forget that you need the Savior's disciples. Some people act as if they can
go it all alone, but God has created us with a need for one another, and we
are designed with interdependence on one another. As brothers in Christ, we
should be there to lend helping hands to one another.

Forsake Not the Assembly

Alden Harden wrote, "It's not good that man should be alone," a recollection from Genesis 2 when God created the first woman to be with
the first man. Eve was God's response to God's declaration. Alden suggested that this was not limited to male-female companionship when
he added, "No matter what the situation may be." Alden reported
being blessed by others, especially his "pen-friends" (see fig. 12.1).

When I requested volunteers for the Death Row sermon project
from the chaplain, Alden was a frequent attendee. I don't know how
he was able to attend so often, as I did not make a special request
for him to be in the writing groups. I worked with three chaplains at
Central Prison whom I asked to provide me with four Death Row
volunteers to write. The chaplains gathered the writers every week,
and the chaplains decided who would attend. Each chaplain did not
know who had attended in prior weeks. It was not a coordinated
effort. I suspect that Alden was frequently making himself available to the three different chaplains, and I was not focused on repeat
participants. The surprise to me happened when I started deciding
which writings to include in the book. The day Alden showed up
to write this piece, he expressed a nervous excitement about having
another chance to tell his story. The topic of this sermon quote was

ideal for Alden because he regularly showed up in the other men's lives on Death Row and prompted them to remain faithful when they started missing the Sunday worship.

Alden's promotion of congregational worship among the men on Death Row indicated to me his belief in assembly. His actions spoke to my heart. There had been times I thought about withdrawing

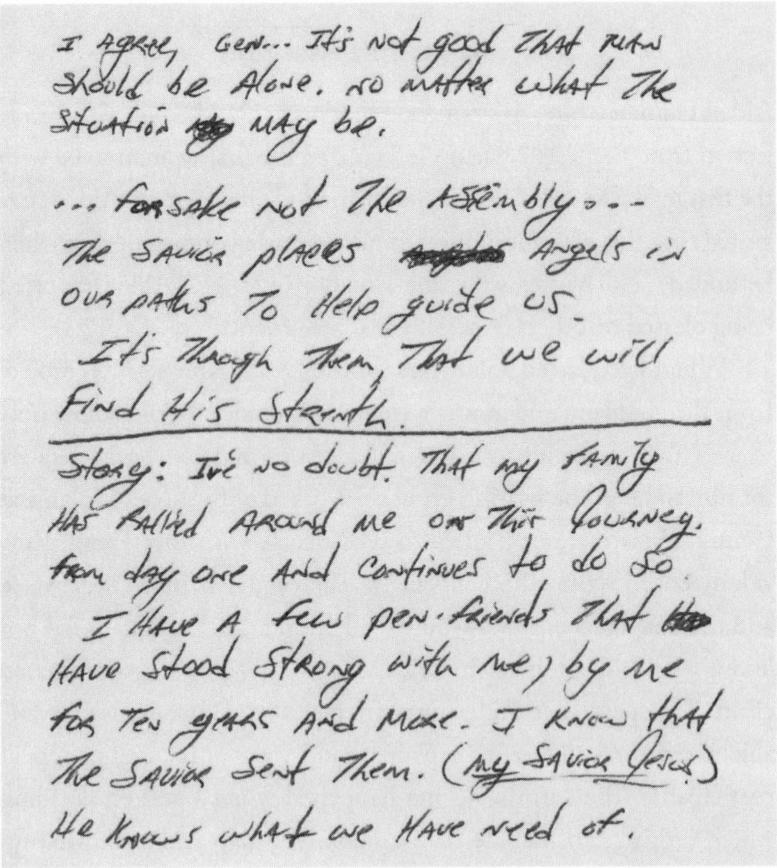

I agree, Gen... It's not good That man should be Alone, no matter what The situation may be.

...forsake not The assembly...
The Savior places Angels in our paths To help guide us.
It's Through Them, That we will Find His strength.

Story: I've no doubt That my family Has Rallied Around me on This Journey. from day one And continues to do so.
I Have A few pen-friends That Have stood strong with me, by me for Ten years And more. I know that The Savior sent Them. (my Savior Jesus)
He knows what we Have need of.

Figure 12.1. Response from Alden Harden

from regular attendance in my church, but Alden helped me stay connected to the local congregation.

My weekly trips to Central Prison occurred at the same time I was being considered as a potential pastor at Mount Bright, since part of me felt it was the same old journey of showing up at a church, displaying my God-given gifts, and facing rejection. Alden's positive tone gave me peace about my candidacy. He helped me see God was in me and was with me. Alden did not like his peers to give up, and I was one of his peers.

God Is Concerned with Our Relationships

George Thomas Wilkerson discussed this practice of supportive participation in one another's lives as a Christian principle taught by Jesus. Jesus indicated that to love God and to love others is the utmost of all the laws. But George went further in his response when he referred to Paul's writings. He wrote, "In 1 Cor. 13 (the love chapter), it lists the features of love. When I look at them closely, I see these define our *relational dynamics*. God is concerned with our relationships! i.e., between Him/us, us/each other" (see fig. 12.2). In other words, without relationships, we are not functional believers. I agree. Relationship with God and with one another is central to what it means to be a Christian.

George took his idea a step further to a challenge that is present in all people. We divide ourselves into packs of "us" versus "them." George inferred that this separation keeps us from serving those we label as "them." He wrote that when we maintain an us-versus-them pattern of thinking and acting, we create fake barriers that hold "them" away.

George also shared how we must be able to receive support when it is offered. He tapped into a key aspect of how the process works: "Part of being in a relationship is *receiving*. I had to learn to receive, so that we can be one, and balanced; not *two*, in an asymmetrical relationship." George meant that in asymmetrical relationships, one person or one group holds all the power and authority over another person or group.

On Death Row, the correctional officers and prison staff have authority. The incarcerated do not decide what time to get up, go to bed, or move from one station to another. Those in authority call all the shots. In this way, the culture on Death Row is like society. We each must realize who has authority over us and whom we have authority over.

The parent/child relationship is the first place this concept is learned. As children mature, parents relinquish authority and children take on more responsibility. In society, there are those who guide or structure behaviors: police, teachers, administrators, officials, etc. On Death Row, the authority is resolute and harsh.

One temptation for the Christian is to gain authority based on servanthood. This method of gaining authority is rooted in the teachings of Jesus Christ. He said, "The greatest among you will be your servant" (Matthew 23:11). Oddly, this teaching includes a virtue of greatness related to being a Christian servant. One could assume that being a servant or giver is a higher classification in the kingdom of God than being a receiver. An artificial haughtiness can creep into the psyche of believers when they resist attempts to be blessed because they want to be givers. When we use phrases like "greatest among you," we take the blessing out of the Creator's hands and put it into our own. A form of self-idolatry can occur because we see ourselves as the source of blessings and not the receivers of blessings.

I agree. The greatest commandments are to love God with our all, and to love one another as ourselves. In 1 Cor. 13 (The love chapter), it lists the features of love. When I look at them closely, I see these define our relational dynamics. God is concerned with our relationships! : i.e., between Him/us, us/each other. We are all part of something greater than ourselves, and can only fully realize that reality — come into our destined and created purpose — by laying down our "I" mentality, by discarding the "Us Vs Them" attitude, and instead embracing the US reality. We are meant to be ONE. period.

Story

I am a brother, a son, a friend, etc. Each of these relational ~~dyna~~ dynamics requires that I express a specific aspect of my love, like light shining through different lenses — and for them to do the same. God says it is more blessed to give than receive. I tend to be a giver, but one day I was in need. A brother noticed and asked if he could get me anything. I told him "no". He said, "Why would you deny me my blessing? You give to others, and it's from the heart, yet you're too proud to receive?" I was convicted because although I thought I was doing good by helping others, I realized part of being in a relationship is receiving. I had to learn to receive, so that we can be one, and balanced; not two, in an asymmetrical relationship.

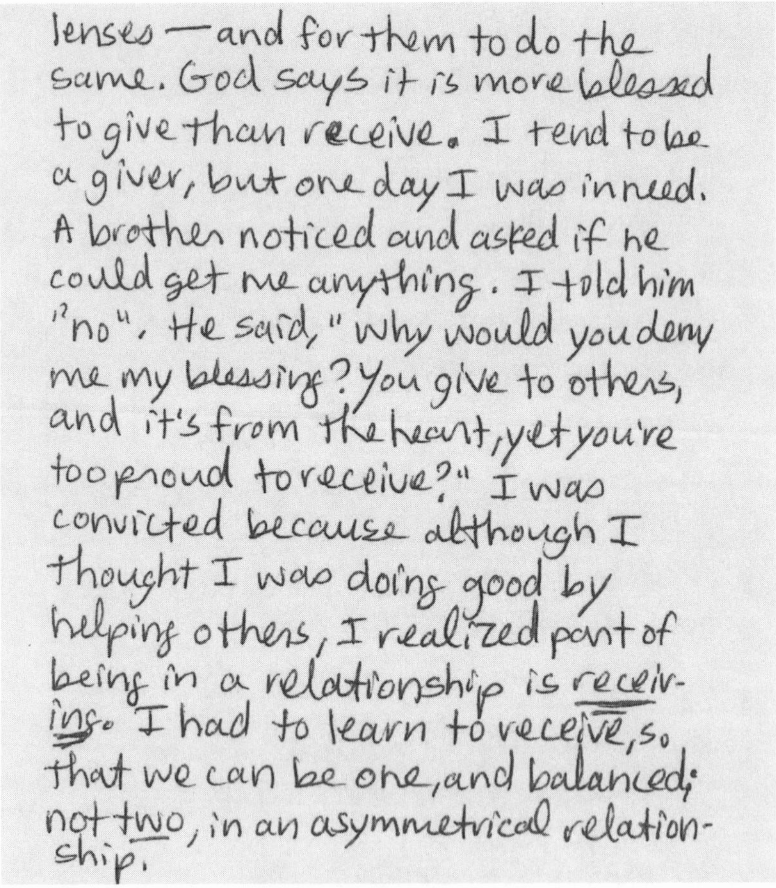

Figure 12.2. Response from George Thomas Wilkerson

Following this logic, George's words touched me deeply when he wrote, "One day I was in need." His confession humbled me because there have been many days that thought I was sufficient to be a husband, father, preacher, teacher, or just a man. My joy came when I could confess that I needed to receive from others if I were going to make any of my relationships and roles effective.

We Need Those Who Will Lead and Comfort Us

Keith East opened another discussion regarding blessings and our innate need for other people. This need supersedes our times of shortages. He declared, "When trying to go it alone we often turn

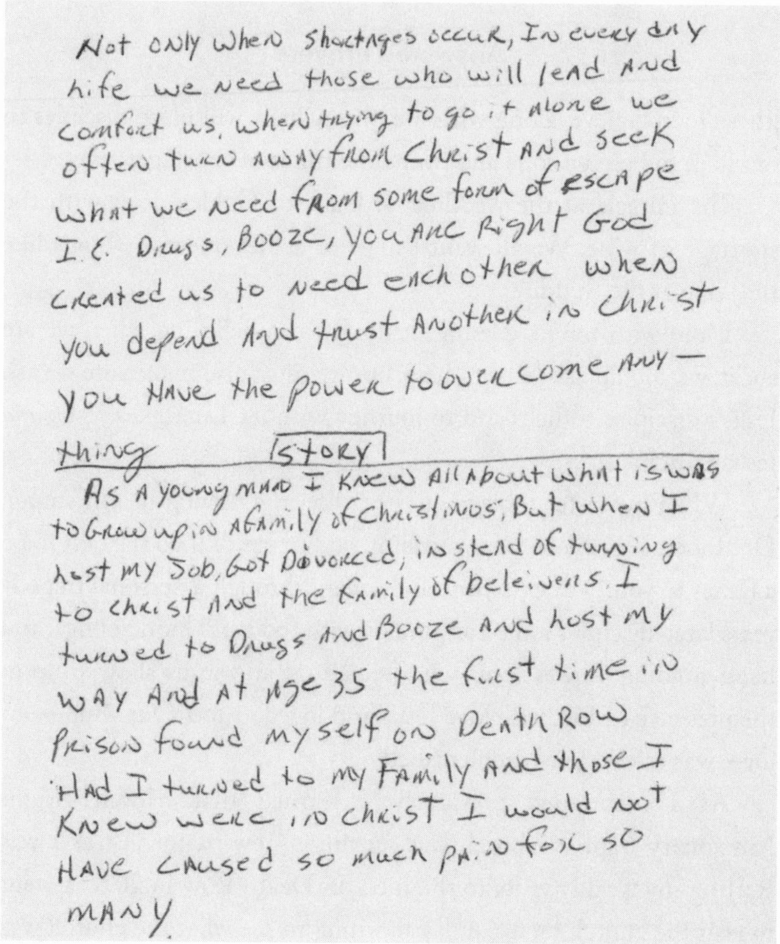

Not only when shortages occur, In every day life we need those who will lead And comfort us. when trying to go it alone we often turn away from Christ And seek what we need from some form of escape I.E. Drugs, Booze, you Are Right God created us to need each other when you depend And trust Another in Christ you Have the power to overcome Any—thing   [Story]

As a young man I knew All About what is was to Grow up in a family of Christians, But when I lost my Job, Got Divorced, instead of turning to christ And the family of beleivers. I turned to Drugs And Booze And lost my way And at age 35 the first time in prison found myself on Death Row Had I turned to my family And those I knew were in Christ I would not Have caused so much pain for so many.

Figure 12.3. Response from Keith East

159

away from Christ and seek what we need from some form of escape, i.e., drugs, booze. You are right, God created us to need each other. When you depend and trust another in Christ you have the power to overcome anything" (see fig. 12.3). His written story demonstrated his regret of not turning for help.

Answered Prayers

These men believe, along with me, that Christ will place disciples in our lives to help us cope and overcome times of shortage.

The miracle at the wedding in Cana of Galilee dealt with the shortage of wine. We all want things or achievements—things like the wine at the wedding.

I join with the people on Death Row in believing when we are short, we should ask Jesus to help, but we must also make sure we ask Jesus's disciples to help and to journey with us. Life takes Jesus *and* Jesus's disciples.

When my sister took my father's life in a mental health stupor, Dr. Robert H. Wilson Sr., my pastor, said to me, "I'll do my best to be a father to you." When Lynne and I went through a personal tragedy years later, disciples rallied around us with food and money, hugs, and hand-holding. It was Jesus who helped us, and Jesus showed up in the presence of folk who love Jesus and loved us too. Our wine—our joy—was miraculously replenished.

As I mentioned previously, I learned that Mount Bright Missionary Baptist Church was seeking a new pastor just as I was starting my weekly visits to the men on Death Row in 2017. I went to visit the church on a Sunday morning to see what the church was like. I was impressed by many things I experienced. The people were warm and friendly. The building and property were kept well. They used the type of technology that churches their size often don't or can't. But what impressed me the most was their deacon's morning prayer. He said, "Lord, we need a pastor. Send us a pastor."

His prayer request spoke volumes about the heart of the deacon. He acknowledged to God that his congregation had a need, and that need would be filled through another person. Their spiritual wine was running low, and one of Jesus's helpers was needed. As I heard him pray, I prayed in silence, *Lord, send me to the right people.* As Mount Bright found me, and I found Mount Bright, I believe both our prayers were answered as we found joy in community.

THIRTEEN

Selfishness and Joy

In the parable Jesus told of the Prodigal Son, the son sought his portion of his inheritance early. When I preached this story to the men, I pointed out how the impetuous son was driven by selfish pursuits. As this is from a parable—a story made up by Jesus—we do not have many details, just that this boy's only concern was himself. He had no concern for his father or brother, nor did he mention a mother or sisters.

Selfishness is demonstrated when a person is excessively, or perhaps even exclusively, concerned with the self above the community good. The selfish person may border on narcissistic or have exaggerated self-worth.

In most Christian communities, selfishness is a negative characteristic. Many sacred texts warn us against pursuing self-interest over the interest of God. The biblical account of Adam and Eve in the garden of Eden challenged God's guidelines. When the serpent suggested to Eve she eat the forbidden fruit, it was a swell of selfishness by her to entertain disobedience.

Selfishness is a challenge we all face. Do I approach what I want, or do I approach what I understand God wants me to do? Eve faced it in the garden of Eden. Moses faced it as he took the life of an Egyptian. David faced it when he saw another man's wife bathing. Peter faced it the night Jesus was taken into custody. These champions of faith all faced trying moments just as we face them, moments when we must decide whether to be faithful to God's call and direction.

The unending question for believers is: How much is my life about individual fulfillment, and how much is it about pursuing community fulfillment and meeting the needs of others? Larry Crabb and Dan Allender discussed this when they wrote, "The philosophy of individualism, in which nothing is more important than an individual's needs and rights, runs today's world, at least in the West. God's deepest passion, however, seems directed not toward individuals (though he numbers the hair on our heads) but toward individuals-in-community."[39] If we see ourselves as the central driving force of a community, we lose perspective of our place. When we see community needs as more important than our own needs, we are in a mindset to aid.

I was interested in exploring selfishness with the men on Death Row. In prison, they'd had opportunities to reflect on selfishness, in their hearts and by how others had treated them. I was not disappointed by their responses. The men opened up about how selfishness impacted their lives and how selfishness was also a challenge behind the solid walls of Death Row.

Writing prompt for those who are incarcerated:

It was selfish pursuits that led this young man away from his father, and it is selfish pursuits that take you away from God. When you become first, you

> are moving to the far country. When you as an individual say you are first, or
> we as a people say we are first, we are moving away from God and going to
> the far country.

Not Caring About Anyone Else

Archie Billings shared that he was not brought up within the church
and its teachings. Archie wrote, "Growing up I took part in worldly
things" (see fig. 13.1). Archie indicated how this pattern can lead a
person to dangerous outcomes from selfishness when he added, "I
was more concerned with getting high not putting my personal needs
in order . . . I even started to steal to support my habits. I was so far
away from 'God.'" Archie noted how selfishness embedded early in a
child's psyche can lead to a situation where he becomes a detriment
to himself or others.

Selfishness has a way of making reality seem like lies and lies
seem like reality. At the heart of all selfishness is an internal belief

AB

For this it rings true. I coming from a household
that didn't attend worship service or discuss
Religion. While growing up I took part in
worldly things and the more you become
Relaxed in your culture the more comfortable
you become. So by not practicing any type
of Religion I fell farther a way from 'God', not
knowing how much I was damaging my
Relationship with God.

> Story
>
> While I agreed with this is, growing up I started doing drugs and drinking alcohol when I was about eleven years old. After I started I started to fail in school I was more concerned with getting high not putting my personal needs in order. I began seperating myself from family and friends. I even started to steal to support my habits. I was so far away from "God," I knew about him but wasn't putting my trust in him letting him to guide my life, and I ended up hitting rock bottom leading me to prison.

Figure 13.1. Response from Archie Billings

that others cannot meet your needs and that you must take action to get what you desire in life. This belief may or may not be validated by past experiences or reality, but it drives people to seek self-satisfaction, relief, and reward regardless of how others are impacted.

Put and Keep God First

James Jaynes initiated positive thoughts about how to combat the consequences of selfishness. He advocated the need to put God first as the pathway to resisting selfish pursuits. In response to the prompt, he wrote, "I know that when I put and keep God first, all else falls into place. My immediate circumstances might not change but how I respond to them will" (see fig. 13.2). He added, "After I was arrested and came to the Row I got back in church, but fell away again. Only in the last few years have I put God first and now I'm at peace. I might not have all I want but God gives me all I need and many of the 'extras.'"

I agree that selfish [J. J.] pursuits take us away from God. I know that when I put & keep God First, all else Falls into Place. My immediate circumstances might not change but how I respond to them will. I'd rather stay in Gods Country than move to a Country so far away I might not find my way home.

P.s.

I enjoy and appreciate Dewey's passion & compassion when he brings The word.

Story:

I was in the Church of my
G-pa for a couple of years,
but left home at 16. That
ended my outside Church life.
After I was arrested and
came to the Row I got
back in Church, but Fell away
again. Only in the last Few
Years have I put God First
and now I'm at Peace. I
might not have all I want
but God gives me all I need
and many of the "extras".

Figure 13.2. Response from James Edward Jaynes

The essence of sin is when we tell God that what God has provided is not good enough. It is a rejection of divine wisdom and a fostering of adoration of what one can accomplish by oneself. Every time we look away from what we believe God is telling us to do and try to do it our way, we sin. Sin may make us feel good initially, but it kills God-given joy. People may get a momentary thrill from it, but that thrill is fleeting, like a short-lived buzz from alcohol.

God Was There

Melvin White Jr. also expressed the need to put God first and to model the Ten Commandments. Melvin wrote, "Seeking God daily will keep us with a understanding that we need HIM first and people. God (10) Commandments, the first 4 are the relationship between HIM and us, the others 6 are how we should treat each others" (see fig. 13.3). Melvin shared a story from a time before incarceration when he was trapped under a car, thinking he was all alone, but he soon realized that "God was there. Yet still I needed to learn to depend on others too and most importantly God in Christ Jesus."

Generally, when someone says someone else does not meet his or her needs, it is about how the two of them engage with each other. It occurs in families, in our communities, on the job, or in social, civic, or religious settings. People lack faith in one another and will seek self-advantage because they worry other people will fail them. While this happens between people, it also happens when we do not believe that God will meet our needs. When we suspect that God will not satisfy our physical, emotional, and spiritual appetites, we pursue tasting from the well of self-satisfaction.

We Want What We See and What We Desire

Warren Gregory expressed how selfishness can cause us to miss the blessing God has planned. He wrote, "When we believe we want what we see and what we desire, we fall short of what God has in store for us" (see fig. 13.4). Warren called selfish pursuits a falling away from God, which connects selfishness to the fall of humankind from God in the Genesis account of creation. Adam and Eve's disobedience is called "the fall of man" by some theologians and

M.L.W. Jr.

As a man of God, I do agree with this statement. I am a person that doesn't like depending
on people, I want to do it all on my own, people
will disappoint you to often. But then that's me
I've disappoint people I love and they still love
me. So I've learned that seeking one's own
way while not thinking of others, disappoint
others. Who is it that don't what to be loved,
included, ask for their opinion?

Seeking God dayly will keep us with
a understanding that we need HIM first
and people. God Commandments, the first 4 (10)
are the relationship between HIM and us, the
others 6 are how we should treat each others

Jesus said, the commandments can be summed
up in these 2 saying. LOVE the LORD thy God with
everything, and others as you, your self.

Story

I Notice that once I was working on
a car, the car fell on me, I was alone and
I needed some body. But, by God's perfect grace
I notice that I wasn't pin-down by the

170

car, so I was able to worm my way out. Too bad I didn't learn from that situation then, only years late did it take. But I did learn. Along I was, but not along Because God was there, Yet still I needed To learn to depend on others & most importantly God in, Christ Jesus.

Figure 13.3. Response from Melvin White Jr.

Christian doctrines. All people subsequently have had to contend with finding a way back to a relationship with God. Warren highlighted that even though Adam and Eve may have initiated the fall phenomenon, we all as descendants continue to replicate the fall with our selfish pursuits.

Warren Gregory was charged with the first-degree murders, kidnapping, and rape of two women. The jury returned guilty verdicts and recommended that Gregory be sentenced to death for each murder, and the trial judge entered judgments in accordance with the recommendation. The jury also found him guilty of assault with a deadly weapon with intent to kill, inflicting serious injury.[40]

Prodigal Son

My selfish pursuits have often driven a wedge between me and my home and family, which lead to the need for ongoing repairs. Such is

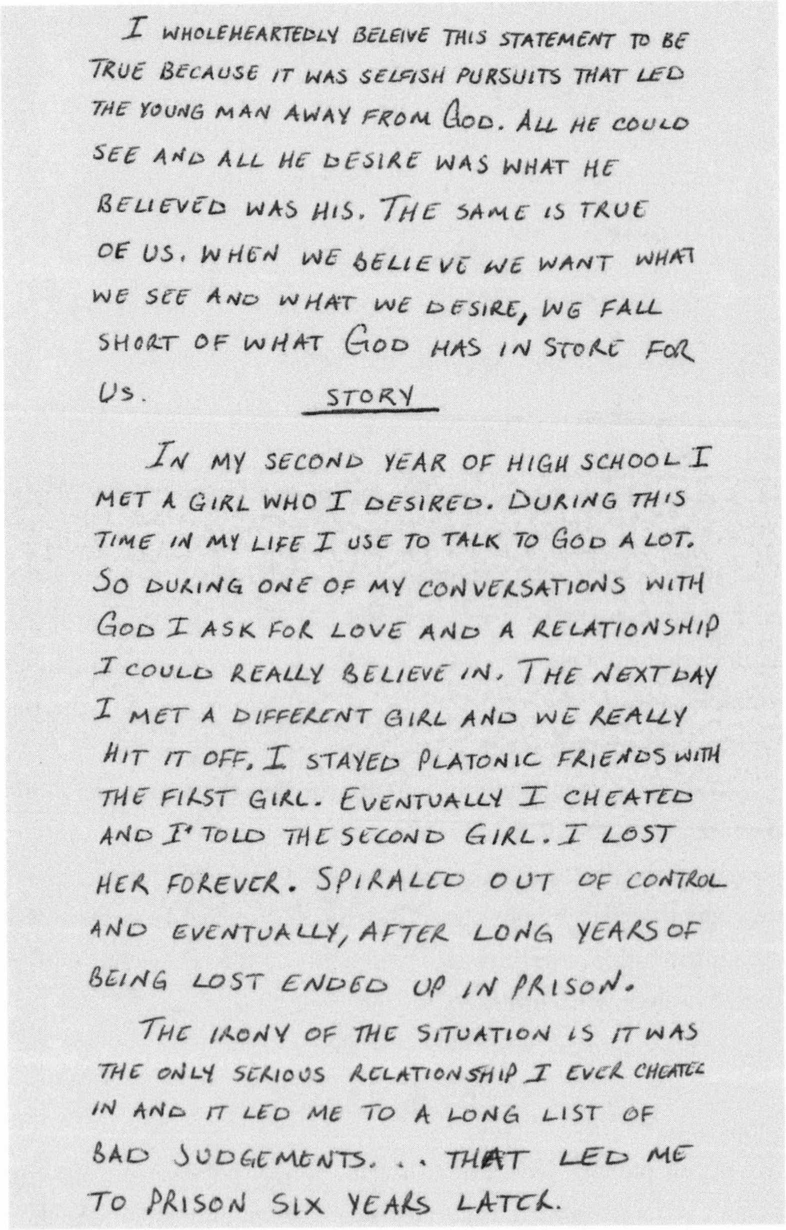

I WHOLEHEARTEDLY BELEIVE THIS STATEMENT TO BE TRUE BECAUSE IT WAS SELFISH PURSUITS THAT LED THE YOUNG MAN AWAY FROM God. ALL HE COULD SEE AND ALL HE DESIRE WAS WHAT HE BELIEVED WAS HIS. THE SAME IS TRUE OF US. WHEN WE BELIEVE WE WANT WHAT WE SEE AND WHAT WE DESIRE, WE FALL SHORT OF WHAT God HAS IN STORE FOR US.

STORY

IN MY SECOND YEAR OF HIGH SCHOOL I MET A GIRL WHO I DESIRED. DURING THIS TIME IN MY LIFE I USE TO TALK TO God A LOT. SO DURING ONE OF MY CONVERSATIONS WITH God I ASK FOR LOVE AND A RELATIONSHIP I COULD REALLY BELIEVE IN. THE NEXT DAY I MET A DIFFERENT GIRL AND WE REALLY HIT IT OFF, I STAYED PLATONIC FRIENDS WITH THE FIRST GIRL. EVENTUALLY I CHEATED AND I TOLD THE SECOND GIRL. I LOST HER FOREVER. SPIRALED OUT OF CONTROL AND EVENTUALLY, AFTER LONG YEARS OF BEING LOST ENDED UP IN PRISON.

THE IRONY OF THE SITUATION IS IT WAS THE ONLY SERIOUS RELATIONSHIP I EVER CHEATED IN AND IT LED ME TO A LONG LIST OF BAD JUDGEMENTS. . . THAT LED ME TO PRISON SIX YEARS LATER.

Figure 13.4. Response from Warren Gregory

the case with all of us. We have done things selfishly that have taken us away from loved ones or friends.

The greater demise occurs when we have selfish pursuits that take us away from God. Our sin will do that. We tell God no when we choose self over God's way, and sin kills joy. But we can have hope that joy can be recovered the same way the Prodigal had joy recovered. We can hope to recover joy the same way these men on Death Row have.

Selfish pursuits for the Prodigal Son took him away from his home and family temporarily. Like him, we can have joy when we go back home to God. Praise God. God always takes us back!

FOURTEEN

Joy Overshadowed

The years of Charity's illness were incredibly taxing. For seven years, we did all we could and spent every dollar we had to try and find out what was happening to our daughter. Her illness and her need for medical treatment added a strain to our already fragile household budget. I was trying to be this strong man at home, in the church, and in the community, but all the challenges I was dealing with were more extensive than my ability to manage. I was failing and failing miserably. Lynne was hurting, and the church was not getting the best it deserved.

One year, I had two season tickets to the Denver Nuggets. The Nuggets were terrible that year, and they were practically giving season tickets away. Charity and I went to most of the games together. It was our father-daughter outlet that I will treasure forever. She was our constant at home as she tried to make it easy on us by cooking and cleaning. She helped Lynne with the church's music and was our congregation's source of joy. Her smile and disposition of peace permeated everyone who was a regular at Abundant Life Baptist Church.

Charity Nicole Williams, age sixteen, in Denver, Colorado.

She did not have many seizures at church, but on one occasion, it was at the church's annual Christmas program. Lynne had prepared a quality musical for everyone to enjoy. One of the songs featured Charity singing a solo with her crystal-clear soprano voice. The church was more packed than it had ever been before, with people standing along the walls. During her solo, Charity had a seizure and collapsed at the front of the church. A seizure is always traumatic for those attending to the one having it, but having an audience focused on it seemed to magnify the event. Everybody wanted to do something, but there was nothing to do but pray and hold one another as Lynne and I held our daughter.

On June 29, 2004, Charity spent the evening with her cousin and friends and came in after I had gone to bed. We had turned the basement of our three-story townhome into a separate apartment for her so she would have her own space. I arose the following day and started my day with a quick breakfast. Lynne had already gone to work, and I was getting ready to go to the church. I hadn't heard any noises from the basement, so I opened the basement door to tell Charity I was leaving. I called down and did not get a response. I started to think that maybe she stayed the night with her cousin. I went downstairs and looked in her room. She lay facedown and motionless in her bed. I called her name again, but there was no response. I reached to wiggle her foot, but her body was cold, and her skin felt stiff. I went to the head of the bed. Her lips were a faint blue, and when I touched her face, it was cold too.

I knew she was dead. An empty feeling hit me at the bottom of my gut. My baby was gone. When Charity first started having seizures, I constantly worried that she could have a seizure, fall, and die from hitting her head on something. It had been years since I worried about her dying; she'd had hundreds of seizures without injury.

I called 911 and was quickly connected with an emergency operator who calmly discussed the situation with me. When I told her Charity's body was cold, she said emergency services were on their way, but they would not have their sirens on. She informed me not to touch her body anymore and not to touch anything in the room. I was told to go to the door and wait for the police and emergency staff to arrive. I went upstairs and went to the door. I immediately called Lynne and said, "I need you to come home right now." She asked me why, and I told her, "Just come home." She said okay, and we hung up.

It seemed like it was a long time that I stood at the door waiting by myself. I am sure it was only a few minutes, but I was alone, and being alone tends to lengthen time out. Suddenly two police arrived with paramedics. The paramedics and one of the police officers went downstairs to Charity's room. The other officer stayed with me to get my statement. Then the coroner and a couple more police cars arrived. I guess when there is a death, they must eliminate the possibility that a crime occurred, before the death can be classified as a medical death or accident, or one from natural causes.

When Lynne arrived home, police and paramedic vehicles were outside our door. She came in, panicked, asking what was going on. I told her, "Charity is gone." Lynne looked at me like she didn't understand what I was saying, then it fully hit her that Charity had died. Like that time in the Mississippi motel when we first saw Charity have a seizure, Lynne collapsed in my arms, but this time she fell all the way to the floor, yelling, "No! No! No!" Tears flowed from her eyes, and wails poured out from the deepest place in her soul. This was now the saddest day in my life. Charity had died, and Lynne's pain could not be consoled.

I lifted Lynne from the floor, and with my arms wrapped around her, I walked her to our sofa. We sat, both crying, with nothing we could say and nothing we could do. While all of this was going on, the coroner came upstairs and indicated that it looked like she'd had a seizure. Since he did not see any reason for the police to be involved, they would bring her body upstairs, and he recommended that we go up to our bedroom because most people don't want to see the bodies of their loved ones carried out. We went to our bedroom, crying and waiting for them to finish.

If there ever was a person who embodied joy, it was Charity. From her birth to her death on June 30, 2004, she added joy to the lives of people she met by simply offering her smile, a kind word, or a funny line. The day she was born, I saw the new bundle of life God had given us. Lynne handed her to me. As a newborn, she opened her eyes wide and looked at me as if she were saying, "What's next?"

Our daughter Tiffany came into town the day after Charity's death, and a couple of days later, Tiffany and Lynne were going through Charity's things when they discovered Charity's diary. None of us knew she was keeping it. She did not journal every day, but on May 27, thirty-four days before she died, she made a profound statement that impacted us and many who knew her. Charity had applied for Social Security disability benefits. For over two years, we had been helping her with the task of applying for benefits and, after being denied, appealing the decision. On May 27, the appeals judge did not deny her appeal but said he needed more evidence to decide. Charity was crushed that the judge did not grant her disability approval.

On that date, she wrote these words in her diary:

There have been times lately when I get frustrated about different things. It could be about this judge I have for SSI stuff who's trying to be as cheap as possible. Sure, I want to take that frustration out on him, but I know that won't help my situation. So, I say, "Hallelujah anyhow." My frustration could be about the doctors who don't know what to do and tell me that they've run out of options. But if I had seizures regularly, I'd be doing a whole lot worse than I am now. So, I say, "Hallelujah anyhow."

I may get frustrated about my memory loss. Sure, there are folk who are surprised that I have no recollection of who they are. But if I was doing a lot worse, I'd most likely not remember my family. I can't fathom that. I thank God for giving me the strength to keep me from losing my memory completely. "Hallelujah anyhow." So, whatever I go through, either good or bad, I'll say "Hallelujah anyhow!"

We published this journal entry in the program for Charity's funeral, which over 900 people attended. Many on the program quoted her by saying, "Hallelujah anyhow." For weeks following the funeral, I would come across someone in Denver, and they would encourage me by saying, "Hallelujah anyhow." Even in Charity's death, she found a way to add joy to my life.

Charity's Death Weighs Heavy

Concurrent with Charity's illness, I became president of the Baptist Ministers' Conference of Metropolitan Denver. We engaged in a major successful project of holding simultaneous revivals across the city. I became the community chair of Denver's Family-to-Family initiative, and we launched a $2 million campaign to reform child welfare. I became the site coordinator of the East Denver Collaboration, and I headed up the service through one of the best-known nonprofits in Denver. I pastored a growing church, and I wanted to expand our facility to accommodate more people. All these factors became a disastrous combination of events in my life.

My desire to expand the church building was more about me than anyone else. Yes, the congregation wanted the project, but I was the main force behind the major renovation that would turn our fifty-seat facility into one that could seat one hundred. I pushed and got funding with a manipulative individual funder who was not friendly to the church or me once we had the funding. He pressed us for payments and made it impossible to refinance the loan.

We were packing out our fifty-seat facility, and I sincerely believed that once all the renovations were completed, our church would attract more than what we had been seeing. During this significant renovation, the city required us to put in an additional basement exit that we had not planned on. The overrun cost made it so the contractor would not finish, and our funder squeezed us harder for payments, though we were renting another facility at the same time. While all of this was happening, Charity died, and our entire congregation mourned her loss. The hope of a renovated building became small compared to our grief.

Our spinning world seemed to intensify, and the fabric of my marital and church life was being ripped apart at the time of Charity's death. Following Charity's death, Lynne started saying she wanted to move to North Carolina to be near our other daughter, Tiffany's new husband, and hopefully one day, our grandchildren. I was resistant to this idea, as I wanted the efforts I had started working on at the church and the community to flourish and succeed. I did not want to leave Denver with "Defeated and Dejected" stamped on my résumé.

Lynne and I had started therapy at Heart of God Counseling to help us cope with all the difficulties we were facing. I remember sitting one evening in a session with our therapist, Deb Lawson, discussing my resistance to the move. Deb said to me, "What do you think would happen if you let go of everything and you fell to the bottom? Do you think you would find God there?"

I remember pontificating an acceptable theological answer to this unthinkable hypothetical forecast. I said what any good preacher would say: "Yes, God is everywhere, so God would be there." My answer was fluffy theological jargon—not something I had pondered. Later that night, I found myself seriously examining how to surrender my ministerial ambitions as the way to provide for my wife. We planned our move from Denver, Colorado, to Durham, North Carolina, for nine months.

FIFTEEN

Joy Within

The day I preached to the men on Death Row about the Prodigal Son, we tried to imagine what a place of joy the father's home was—a place where the son was loved and all his provisions were met. After his selfishness led him to take his inheritance and flee to the far country, he spent his money and then, during a nationwide famine, took a job feeding pigs. With no family, friends, or provisions, joy had become a distant memory. The Bible says he became destitute enough to contemplate eating pig slop (Luke 15:11–32).

The sermon quote I gave them as a writing prompt plays with the language regarding the pig's food, and it suggests a common problem that everyone has when they reach a low point in their lives. The Prodigal Son was tempted to do what he would normally consider disgusting. Jesus told this story to a Jewish audience, a people who didn't consume pigs. Everyone knew pigs lived in squalor, and their granular meals became mingled with their filth. No person who valued their human dignity would eat such slop.

The pig slop also had little nutritional value. In terms of emotional and spiritual intake, we may get to a point where we think junk is all there is left for our minds and souls. Donald G. Hanna is a policeman, teacher, and author. He was a police chief for twenty-four years in two Illinois cities and at Ohio State University. In his book *Mastering Self,* he stated:

> We live in a culture that is mostly junk: an appropriate, descriptive term for shallow, superficial appeal or utility that lacks substance. Junk is insignificant. So the term fits in describing much in our culture. Junk promotes mediocrity: junk books, junk music, junk art, junk movies, and junk entertainment all promote junk thinking, junk interests, junk beliefs, junk values, junk priorities, and a junk mindset. This mental disposition is a preoccupation with self.[41]

The Prodigal was ready to devalue himself and consume the pig's chow. His thinking was like the men on Death Row. Death Row is a modern-day pigpen that drastically limits their physical choices as well as their spiritual and emotional freedom. They feel they must eat spiritual and emotional "pig food" presented to them by the prison system, by correctional staff, or by other men who are incarcerated.

Writing prompt for those who are incarcerated:

You are locked up physically behind bars, and your body is forced to comply with the rules of the State. But hear me: Your mind and your spirit are free, and you don't have to consume with your mind and your spirit what the pigs are consuming.

Reading the Word of God

Iziah Barden associated the freedom of mind and spirit with the awareness of finding ways to learn even while behind bars. To Iziah, a receptive mind was a key that unlocked the door to a freed spirit. He contributed to this concept: "One must keep learning and listing to be aware of what's happing today and all around" (see fig. 15.1).

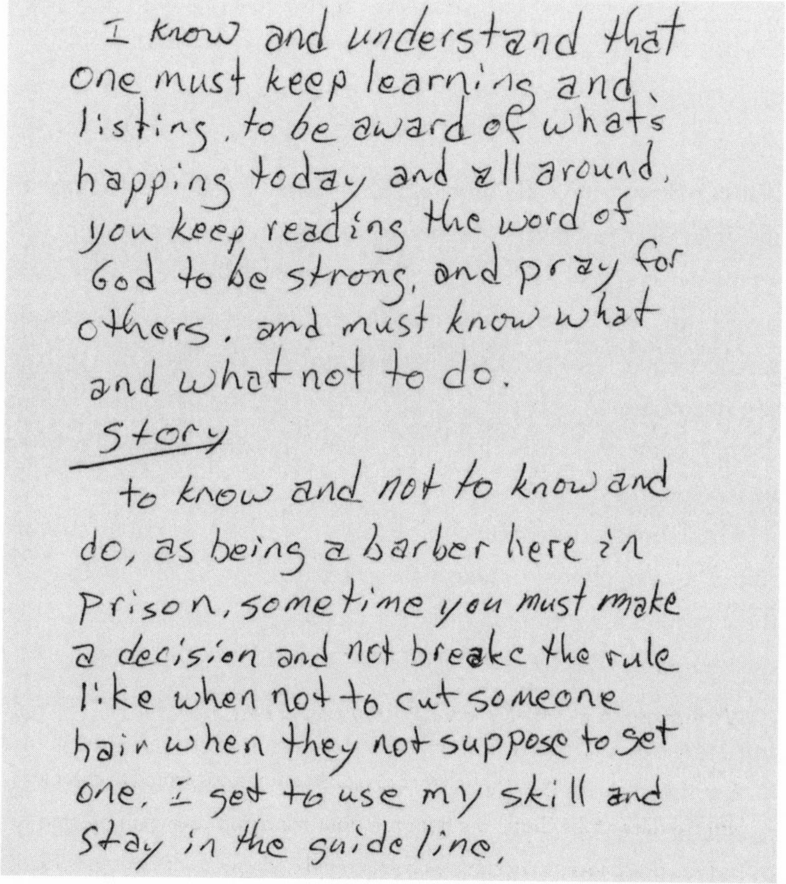

> I know and understand that one must keep learning and listing, to be award of whats happing today and all around. you keep reading the word of God to be strong, and pray for others, and must know what and what not to do.
>
> Story
>
> to know and not to know and do, as being a barber here in Prison, sometime you must make a decision and not breake the rule like when not to cut someone hair when they not suppose to get one, I get to use my skill and stay in the guide line,

Figure 15.1. Response from Iziah Barden

He said he believed in reading the Word of God. He continued, "You keep reading the word of God to be strong, and pray for others, and must know what and what not to do."

Iziah Barden was indicted for first-degree murder and robbery. In November 1999, he was found guilty, and at his sentencing proceeding, the jury recommended the death penalty. The court entered the recommended judgment for the first-degree murder conviction while rendering a stay of judgment on armed robbery conviction.[42]

The Positive Road

Nathan Bowie made a point regarding what I believe to be one of the great human powers: the power to choose. True freedom occurs after a person chooses to be free. Nathan wrote, "While in prison you have a choice to be positive or not. There are many positive things you can do in here" (see fig. 15.2). Nathan stressed that even in a restrictive maximum-security facility, he has choices. As mentioned before, Nathan came to Death Row for a double murder committed when he was twenty years old.

Those incarcerated can choose to go to worship or not go to worship. They can choose to take a class or not. They can choose to go to the common area in their assigned POD or stay in the room. They can choose to read the provided books or not.

We all have choices to make, too, and our choices can lead us *into* freedom and joy or *away* from freedom and joy. Choice is one of our great tools. Nathan also wrote, "Many times over the years people have tried to get me off the positive road. Its a struggle but, I always remember that it is my choice. Everyone has to make that choice for themselves."

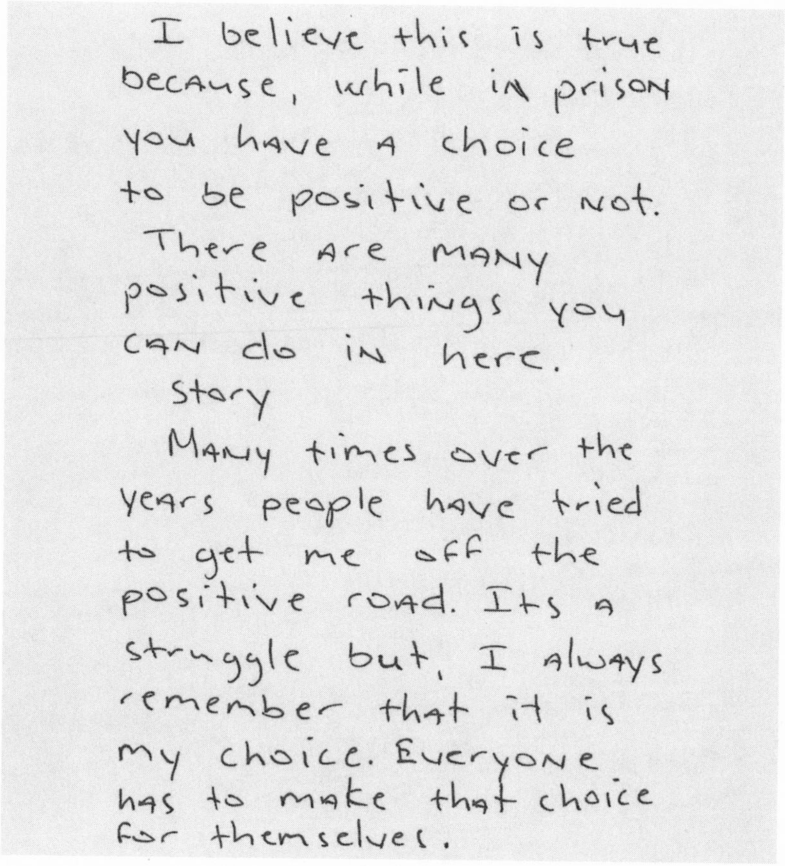

> I believe this is true
> because, while in prison
> you have a choice
> to be positive or not.
> There are many
> positive things you
> can do in here.
>   Story
>   Many times over the
> years people have tried
> to get me off the
> positive road. Its a
> struggle but, I always
> remember that it is
> my choice. Everyone
> has to make that choice
> for themselves.

Figure 15.2. Response from Nathan Bowie

He Is with Me Now

"I'm freer in here behind these walls locked up, then I was before I came to prison. Not physically but spiritually." These words from Stephen Buckner shook me. I reread them several times. Stephen struck at the core of freedom's power. He declared that physical locations have barriers and restraints for the body, but the mind can wander, stroll, and even march beyond those barriers.

I've all ready found out, I'm freer in
here behind these walls locked up,
then I was before I came to prison.
Not physically but spiritually. I've
also learned to be content whether
I've little or alot. I walk everyday
with my Saviour, and I know he is
ever present with me. I've been
blessed here in prison with Sunday
Services, Tuesday Bible Study and
Thrusday Discipleship Class. I also
have Christian brothers who help me
too! So yes I'm free in spirit and
mind. I do have the joy, peace,
and hope in Jesus Christ.

Story
I was going down a dark road
outside of here. I was doing
things that was breaking
God's laws, and then men (society)
laws. The result of this road
lead me here. It was there at

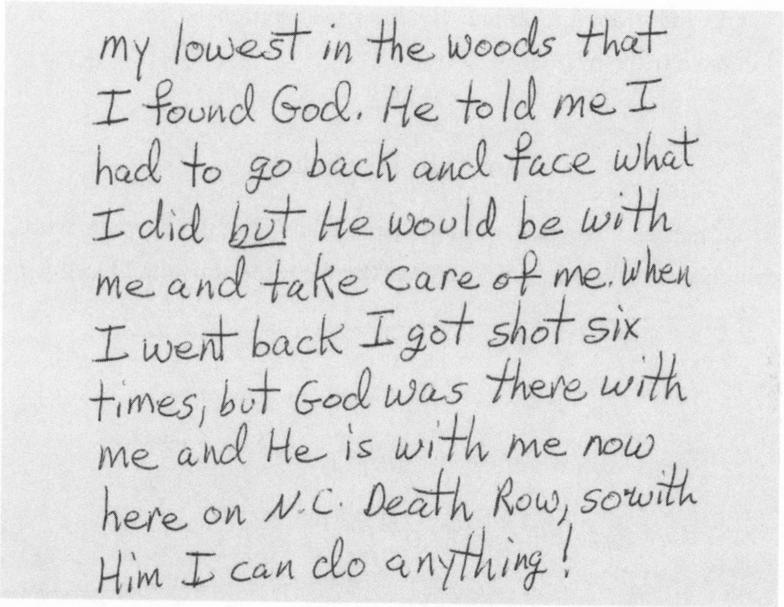

my lowest in the woods that I found God. He told me I had to go back and face what I did but He would be with me and take care of me. When I went back I got shot six times, but God was there with me and He is with me now here on N.C. Death Row, so with Him I can do anything!

Figure 15.3. Response from Stephen Buckner

Stephen suggested that the freedom he had before incarceration had a different type of restraint. He was trapped on roads that took away his freedom of spirit. He described his life before he was locked up as a "dark road" (see fig. 15.3). Stephen stated that people can be incarcerated in their minds, and their behaviors can be restricted, but we can all find ways for our minds and spirits to be free.

Stephen provided us with a clue to how he has developed a sense of freedom while on Death Row: in Christian fellowship and discipleship. Listen to what he said about his spiritual life: "I walk every-day with my Saviour, and I know he is ever present with me. I've been blessed here in prison."

As mentioned, Stephen Buckner was sentenced to death for a domestic triple murder.

I Am Truly Free in Jesus

In an earlier chapter, I quoted Terry Alvin Hyatt, the man whose responses on the wine shortages at the wedding in Cana of Galilee I

> My sprit was bound in the world when I thought I was free. But I know that I locked up I am truley free In Jesus my Lord. My berden is now my blessing. Because I fockes on my Lord Jesus and not on myslef. I am truley free in him.
>
> Story
> Freedom is not allways being Free

Figure 15.4. Response from Terry Alvin Hyatt

wrote down for him. At the time he wrote about joy within, he was new to reading and writing.

Terry, who was sentenced for kidnapping, rape, and murder, made a profound statement. He wrote, "My spirit was bound in the world when I thought I was free. But now that I locked up I am truley free in Jesus my Lord . . . Freedom is not all ways being Free" (see fig. 15.4). He, like so many of those on Death Row, saw his incarceration as an unexpected pathway to spiritual freedom. Through Terry's statement, we learn a person can be free in places when the rest of society views them as incarcerated.

Mind Over Matter

Warren Gregory introduced a theoretical special relationship to the issue of being physically locked up but being spiritually free. Warren used the common phrase "mind over matter," which he indicated can make a difference in your life (see fig. 15.5). He reflected on how

> THIS STATEMENT IS TRUE AND IT IS REALER THAN MOST PEOPLE THINK. IT IS ALL MIND OVER MATTER!
>
> I ONCE HEARD IT SAID THAT THE GREATEST THING IN THE HANDS OF THE OPPRESSORS IS THE MINDS OF THE OPPRESSED. SINCE HEARING THAT I FOCUS MY MIND AND MY THOUGHTS ON BETTERING MYSELF, REGARDLESS OF MY SITUATION.

<u>STORY</u>

THERE WAS A TIME WHEN I WAS MUCH YOUNGER THAT I WOULD ALWAYS LISTEN TO WHAT OTHER THOUGHT OF ME. THEN AFTER A GREAT DEAL OF MENTAL AND SPIRITUAL GROWTH I REALIZED, IT MATTERS NOT WHAT OTHERS THINK OF ME, OR WHAT THEY THINK I SHOULD DO, OR HOW I SHOULD ACT. WHAT MATTERS MOST IS WHAT I THINK AND THAT MY THOUGHTS AND ACTION REFLECT MY MENTAL AND SPIRITUAL GROWTH.

Figure 15.5. Response from Warren Gregory

we can be led into consuming what others are consuming because we fear the backlash if we don't kowtow to others. In other words, peer pressure pushes people toward "pigpen" practices. Read Warren's words about not consuming what the pigs consume because you are free in your mind and spirit.

Howard Thurman, perhaps our country's greatest twentieth-century theologian, discussed how true freedom must be a personal discipline. Thurman wrote:

Here we come upon the most interesting aspect of personal freedom—the living of one's life with confidence that transcends discouragement and despair. This means that one does not have to depend upon the favorable circumstance, the fortuitous "break," the applause, approval, and felicitation of friends, important as these are. The secret is the quiet inner purpose and the release of vitality with which it inspires the act. Achieving the goal is not measured by some external standard, though such must not be completely ignored. Rather, it is measured in terms of loyalty to the purpose and the freedom which it inspires.[43]

Warren Gregory's mind and spirit remain free even though his body is caged behind thick cement, steel doors, and wired fences. His writings expressed what true freedom is all about.

My Joy Transformation

My personal story is one of finding myself low in the pigpen—ready to eat, if not outright already eating, what the other pigs were eating. I always wanted to be the guy who fit in or shared the spotlight of popularity. I wanted to be the guy whom girls found appealing and boys considered cool. As a young adult, I wanted to be a student who was bright, witty, and scholarly, though I was not the student who could impress teachers or my peers. As a preacher, I wanted to be thought-provoking with charismatic zeal, able to captivate church folk. I wanted all of this for the wrong reasons. I wanted selfish admiration as opposed to a God-delivered word that touched people's lives.

Much of my life was spent tasting what the pigs ate until I realized that God has better for me. I realized that if I seek God to feed my soul, I am more effective and powerful as a husband, father, brother, friend, neighbor, and even as a preacher. Not only has God provided better for me, but I am freer in my spirit now than all the days I spent eating metaphorical slop.

My joy was recovered when I realized I could return to God and God's provisions. It came when I realized the men and women on Death Row valued what I shared with them. My joy was the expectancy on their faces when I arrived and the smiles of satisfaction when I left. They were appreciative of my words and I of theirs. We were an answer to one another's prayers.

SIXTEEN

Separation and Joy

A nother sermon I preached in the prison concerned two sto-ries of mother-daughter pairs—one from the Bible, and one modern—who experienced hardship and loss but found joy. During the prayer time, when the liturgist asked if anyone had prayer requests, two men responded with conflicting agendas. Christopher Roseboro asked for prayer as his case was being appealed. With success, he would get off Death Row. James Jaynes asked for prayer for all the victims' families that he and the other men present had harmed.

The contrast between these two requests was remarkable. One was seeking personal benefit to eliminate separation from his family and friends. The other lifted the lives of people who were affected by those murdered at the hands of the men in the room. The first wanted to ease his separation from society. The second wanted to ease the separation of those he did not know. Both requests were genuine and touching.

So, as we joined in a small group, I was interested to see what the other men would write. We discussed the Hebrew Bible story of Naomi and Ruth—a mother-in-law and her daughter-in-law. Naomi was a Hebrew woman, and Ruth was a Moabite woman. Naomi's husband and sons died, including Ruth's husband. The sermon dealt with the absence of joy due to separation by death.

Death caused a permanent separation between these women and their husbands. There would be no more daily talks, evening meals, moments of intimacy, or benefits from the men's income. Naomi and Ruth were cut off from what they wanted and needed from their husbands. The retributive prison system does the same thing to the families of men and women who are incarcerated today. A separation occurs that prevents people who are incarcerated from contributing substantially and meaningfully to their families.

The current retributive justice system in the United States pits the accused perpetrator of a crime against the State. The State pursues a form of revenge toward the accused. Crime victims and their families are brought into an alliance with prosecutors to fight the accused. Typically, prosecutors instruct victims and their families not to contact the accused and the accused's family because it could weaken their chances of getting a conviction. A major compelling argument that prosecutors push the victims to accept is revenge against the individuals they have been determined are perpetrators of the crime.

Loneliness takes its place in the men and women in prison and especially on Death Row. The noise reverberates off the cement walls and steel bars, absent of the sounds of a home where spouses, siblings, parents, and children are present. Perhaps the separation related to being away from children is the strongest sentiment expressed by those incarcerated. In his book *Beyond the Walls of Separation*, Chaplain Tobias Brandner wrote about these feelings that people who are incarcerated often express: "The pain caused by separation from children is experienced as a painful inability to educate them in a good direction, a loss of relation and influence, or powerlessness at witnessing how they too slowly slide into criminal activities."[44]

Since contact with the accused could jeopardize its case, the State opposes the accused and the victim's family coming together in any fashion. As such, the perpetrator's family becomes the enemy as well. Often in court and outside the court, the families of victims sit and stand on opposite sides of the room or hallway. The victim's family often sends ugly glances of hatred toward the perpetrator's family. It is widely known such looks are premeditated and perpetrated by the prosecution as they attempt to prevent any chance of the families making peace.

In their book *Beyond Prisons: A New Interfaith Paradigm for Our Failed Prison System*, Laura Magnani and Harmon L. Wray discussed victim-perpetrator separation: "The system discourages them from feeling or expressing any openness to understanding, meeting with, or reconciling with the designated offender, and discourages them from having anything to do with the defense lawyers. The converse is true as well."[45] Prosecutors desire victims and victims' families to be angry with perpetrators so that the judge or the jury witness an intense pain on their faces, in their body language, and in their words.

The revenge that drives our retributive justice system is not the path that God wants us to take. In the book of Leviticus from Hebrew scriptures, the people are warned about not using revenge as a tool of punishment. It says, "You shall not take vengeance or bear a grudge against any of your people, but you shall love your neighbor as yourself: I am the LORD" (19:18). While this verse is often misinterpreted to imply that God is vengeful, this passage means that vengeance belongs to God, who is merciful—not to the victims' families, and not to society (who will not have mercy) to act on behalf of the victim.

One other group that is also caught by retributive justice is the accused's family. Men and women who are incarcerated are taken away from their spouses, children, parents, siblings, or other family members. Often we fail to recognize that sending a man to prison also forces many families into poverty, onto welfare rolls, out of housing, and out of schools. The accused's family is not forced behind bars and cement walls, but other restrictions are forced upon them. When a breadwinner is no longer in the home due to incarceration, the family's hopes are dashed. In a way, they are locked up by the separation forced between them and the accused perpetrator.

Reading the writings of the men on this quote was the most discouraging of all I read. The men wrote sad stories about their separations from family. They were painful and difficult memories. This sermon and the responses pinpointed how we cope with separation.

The men and women on Death Row never expect to get out of prison. They'll die there when the State takes their lives, unless they die from other causes. The separation is permanent, and the families of those incarcerated will never again have the incarcerated in their homes.

Writing prompt for those who are incarcerated:

Prisons have served punishment—not only on the men incarcerated but also on the loved ones who do not get to benefit from the presence and resources of the men incarcerated. Just like Naomi and her daughters-in-law felt the pain of being separated from their men, prisons can do the same thing to families today.

The Ripple Effect

William C. Gregory, at two separate meetings, wrote about separation from his family and how it impacted him. William was eighteen when he was sentenced to death. He wrote, "Not having physical contact with my family is very hard on both sides . . . All these years

Yes, I believe this statement is True! I've been incarcerated for over 25 yrs now. Twenty-three years I've been on deathrow. I got locked up at 18 yrs old. My siblings were 3 and 1 at the time. I also had a son who was 16 months at the time. So this is devastating to a family on a emotional, financial, mental and physical level. Not having physical contact with my family is very hard on both sides. I can't work on deathrow so it's a strain on my parents financially. All these years have brought anger, disappointment, sadness on the emotional side for us all! So prisons really try to tear the family structure down on those incarcerated!

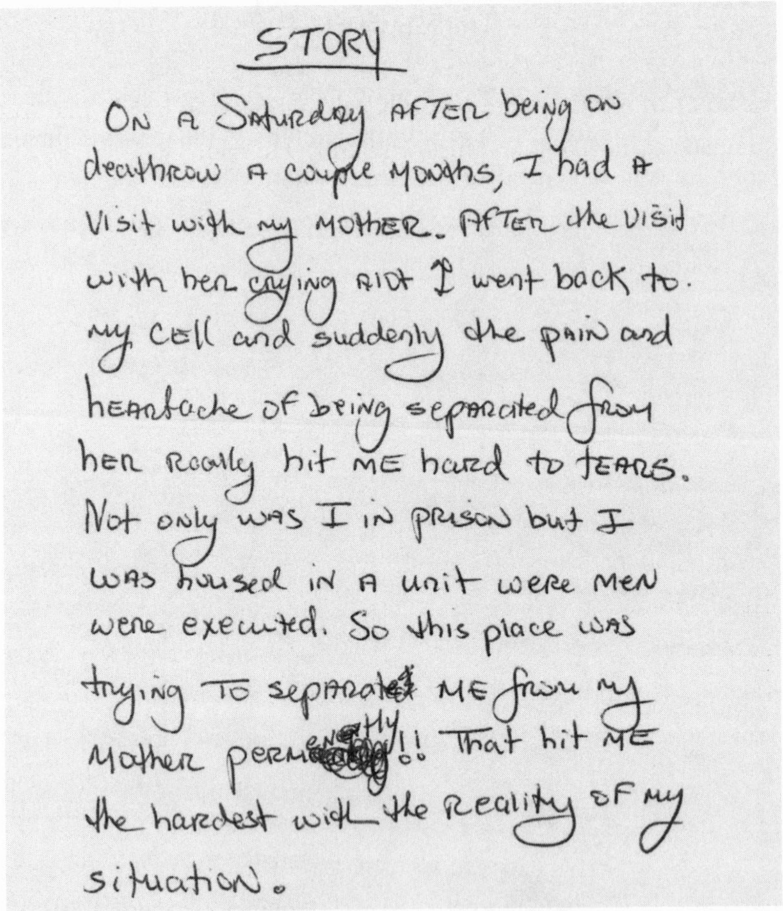

STORY

On a Saturday after being on
deathrow a couple months, I had a
visit with my mother. After the visit
with her crying aird I went back to.
my cell and suddenly the pain and
heartache of being separated from
her really hit me hard to tears.
Not only was I in prison but I
was housed in a unit were men
were executed. So this place was
trying to separate me from my
Mother permanetly!! That hit me
the hardest with the reality of my
situation.

Figure 16.1. First response from William C. Gregory

have brought anger, disappointment, sadness on the emotional side
for us all! So prisons really try to tear the family structure down on
those incarcerated!" (see fig. 16.1). He wrote a heartfelt remembrance
from his early days on Death Row when it hit him that he was separated from his mother permanently.

The second sit-down with William (see fig. 16.2) put in parallel the separation that he inflicted on all the victims of his crime. He spoke of those whom we typically call victims (the family that lost someone at his hand) and his own family. He said:

> When the judge sentenced me to death at 18 yrs of age, not only was I devastated but my immediate family too. My mother, dad, two sisters, my son and grandfather depended on me as well! So I took a precious loved one from the victims family and didn't realize how much pain and suffering my actions caused my own family! *The ripple effect* I caused stretched miles and miles.

In January 1993 William C. Gregory was indicted for first-degree murder, assault with a deadly weapon, and felonious breaking and entering. He was tried and found guilty of all charges in 1994. The jury recommended the death sentence, and William was sentenced in accordance with the recommendation.[46]

As William reflected on his separation from family, he indicated how this happens to many men across the nation. "Now I'm 43 years of age," he wrote, "and my family could really need my financial support as well as moral support. The male figures of America are lost in the prison system. That really effects generations and generations down the road."

James Samuel Logan, professor of religion and African and African American studies at Earlham College, wrote about the failures of prison systems regarding Black men in his book *Good Punishment?* He argued, "When disproportionately large numbers of young Black men are doing time in overcrowded, single-sex, racist,

When the judge sentenced me to death at 18 yrs of age, not only was I devastated but my immediate family too. My mother, dad, two sisters, my son and grandfather depended on me as well! So I took a precious loved one from the victims family and didn't realize how much pain and suffering my actions caused my own family! The Ripple Effect I caused stretched miles and miles. My son was 16 months old, my sisters 3 yrs old & 15 months old. Now I'm 43 yrs of age and my family could really need my financial support as well as moral support. The male figures of America are lost in the prison system. That really effects generations and generations down the road.

Story

At the time I was taking care of my grandfather (I was living with him) and I had a son. I just graduated from high school. So I had responsibilities

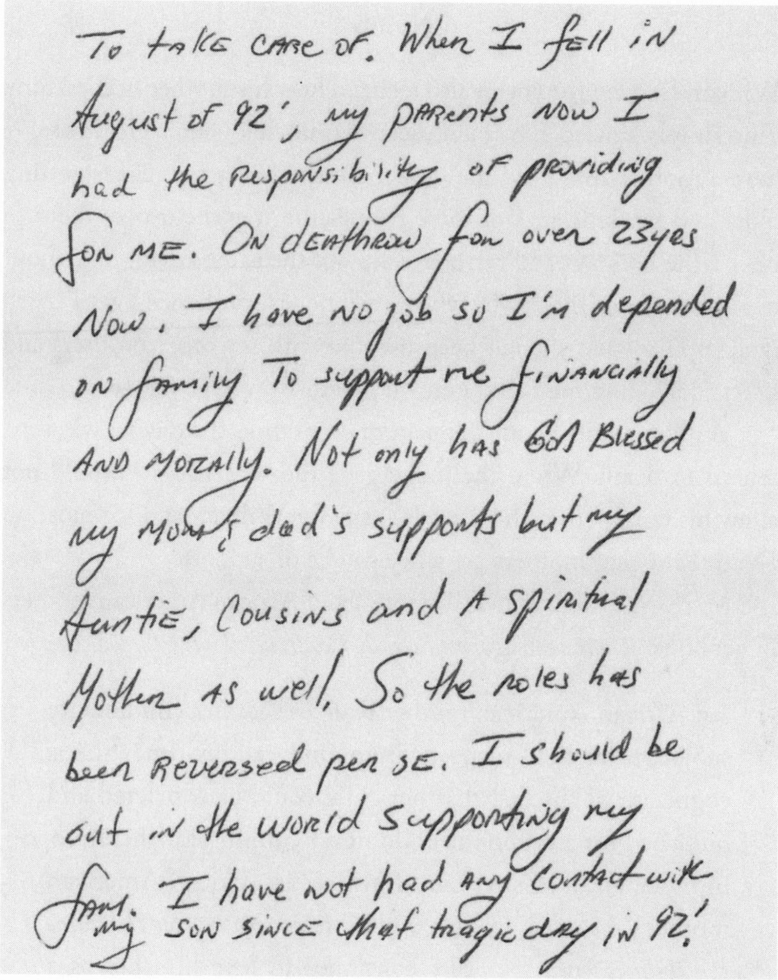

To take care of. When I fell in August of 92', my parents now I had the responsibility of providing for ME. On deathrow for over 23 yes Now. I have no job so I'm depended on family to support me financially And Morally. Not only has God Blessed my Mom's dad's supports but my Auntie, Cousins and A spiritual Mother As well, So the roles has been Reversed per se. I should be out in the world supporting my fam. I have not had any contact with my son since what tragic day in 92'.

Figure 16.2. Second response from William C. Gregory

and routinely violent fortresses of social vengeance and degradation, it is not reasonable then to expect (on balance) positive contributions from them when they return to their communities and to society at large."[47]

Numb

William Eugene Robinson also realized how his mother needed him. This simply caused him pain, deep within his being. He wrote, "I have a mother that need me now more than ever, because is getting older and her kids are not there for her the way she expect them to be . . . The holidays and birthdays are not the same anymore without her kids around. That's why when I call her every chance I get I try to make up for what she has been missing with my other brothers and sisters, including me being here on Death Row" (see fig. 16.3).

William wrote about the pain of separation the day he was sentenced to death. When the judge gave the sentence, he would not allow his family to see his face. It's true for William and for most on Death Row that mothers are a key source of support.

MarKeva Gwendolyn Hill wrote about African American mothers in her book, *Womanism against Socially Constructed Matriarchal Images*:

> An African American mother realizes that her children are subject to be held suspect for anything at any time. She is cognizant of the fact that her child could be convicted and punished for a crime the child never committed. Therefore, to mock an unjust system of justice, an African American mother's response to such violations is, *No matter the crime the child is mine* . . . She continues to love him/her as a whole object and not split with the good child—bad child because of the dominant culture's assessment of, not only her child, but any member of her race. She realizes that the definition of good and bad are constructed and maintained by a system of oppression where dominance, not justice, is the goal.[48]

William wrote twice in response to this sermon. He described the prison system as a wedge—a purposeful and intentional form of separation that occurred between himself and his family. A wedge's usefulness is to push apart two objects, and that is what William saw the prison system doing. He wrote, "Prison life has put a wedge between me and my family. Not being able to keep that connection threw out the years, put a strain on our relationships (out of sight, out of mind)."

I would say that this is true in deed!

The reason being is, I have a mother that need me now more than ever, because is getting older and her kids are not there for her the way she exspect them to be. So when I talk to her on the phone, I can hear it in her voice that she is lonely and sad. The Hoildays and birthdays are not the same any more without her kids around. Thats why when I call her every chance I get I try to make up for what she been missing with my other brothers and sisters, including me being here on Death Row.

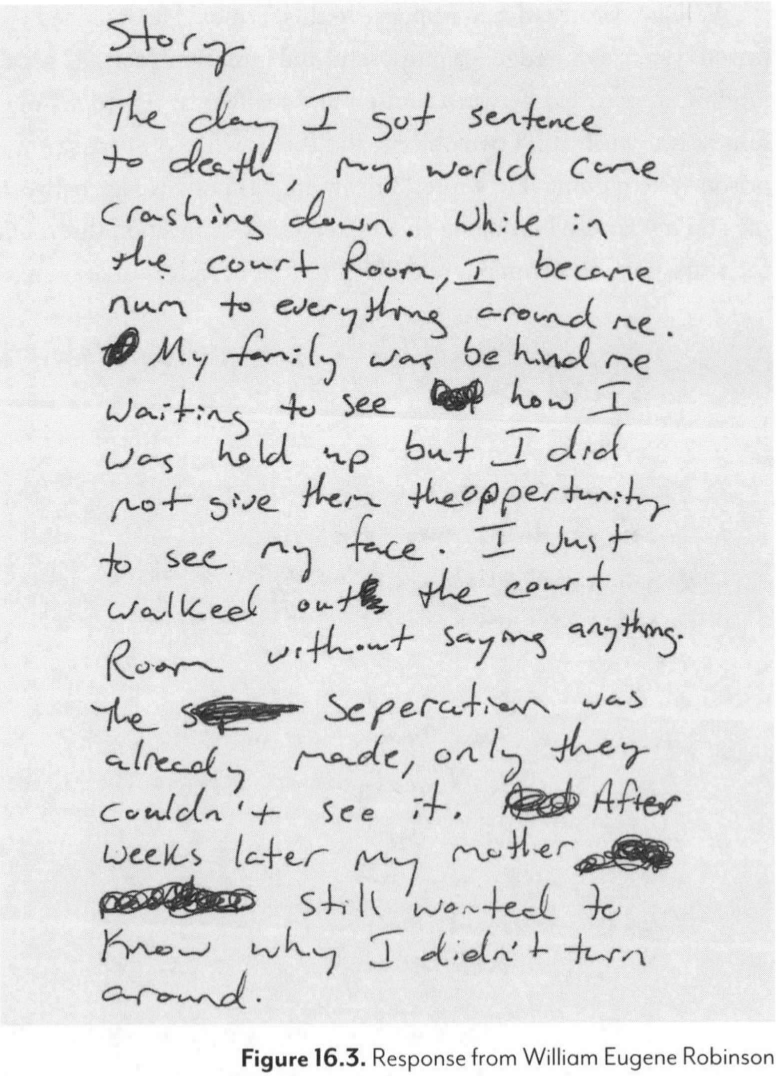

Story

The day I got sentence
to death, my world came
crashing down. While in
the court Room, I became
num to everything around me.
My family was behind me
waiting to see how I
was hold up but I did
not give them the oppertunity
to see my face. I just
walked out the court
Room without saying anything.
The seperation was
already made, only they
couldn't see it. After
weeks later my mother
still wanted to
know why I didn't turn
around.

Figure 16.3. Response from William Eugene Robinson

William shared his pain of separation from his siblings too. The language he chose—"They still say they love me"—indicated he longed for a deeper connection than words can provide. He showed his humanity by expressing a desire to have more genuine contact. In

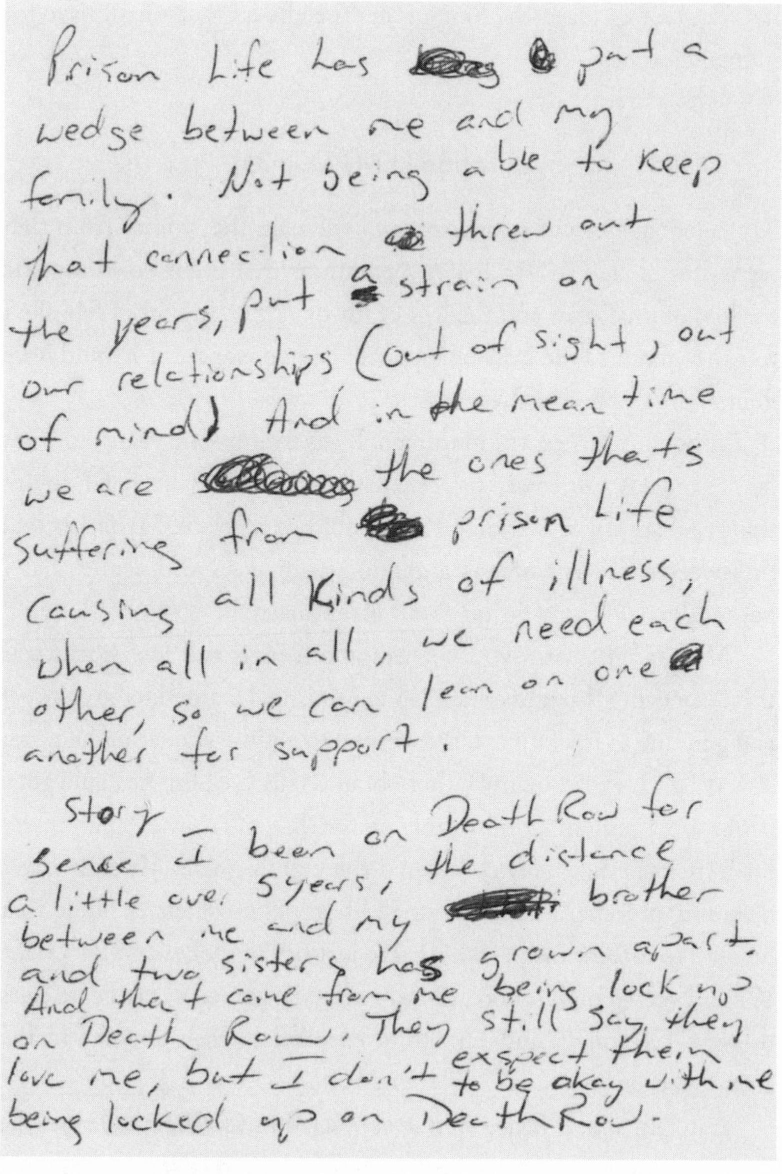

Prison Life has ~~been~~ put a wedge between me and my family. Not being able to keep that connection ~~over~~ threw out the years, put a strain on our relationships (out of sight, out of mind) And in the mean time we are ~~always~~ the ones thats suffering from ~~the~~ prison life causing all kinds of illness, when all in all, we need each other, so we can lean on one another for support.

Story — Sence I been on Death Row for a little over 5 years, the distance between me and my ~~older~~ brother and two sisters has grown apart. And that come from me being lock up on Death Row. They still say they love me, but I don't expect them to be okay with me being locked up on Death Row.

Figure 16.4. Second response from William Eugene Robinson

his way, he expressed the longing and neediness that we all have for mutual closeness.

Separation in My Own Life

My personal story of separation and the pain that comes from that separation is tied to two major separations that occurred in my life: the loss of my father and the loss of my daughter. In both, I felt like I was the victim as the losses happened, I often wonder if I could have done more to prevent these losses.

When my father was murdered, I was twenty-one years old. That family tragedy came with pain that still has not fully healed. I do not want to disrupt the mending that is still taking place. My father had the sweetest spirit and was a genuine man of God. I regret that I never talked with my father about his ministry.

My thoughts of my father were both high and low, but it was these opposing thoughts that inspired my life. I wanted to be as sweet and genuine as my father, but I wanted to get the education he never did. When I was a boy, my father obtained his GED so he could get a better job. I remember him studying for that and how difficult it was for him, as he had only completed the eighth grade. My father was a reading preacher and had a small library at our Denver home that he used to inform his preaching. He just never got beyond his GED. When I was in high school, a local seminary offered a certificate class in New Testament, and my father enrolled himself and me in the class together.

Later in life, I had a better appreciation for the challenges he faced. He was a family man with eight children to raise, eight mouths to feed, and eight bodies to house. Surely it was difficult to work, minister, and go to school. I am the seventh of eight children. If he had chosen to go to school earlier in his life, he might have not had me.

The reality is that my father was a big part of my motivation to get an education and to do well in ministry. When he died, part of my dream to achieve what he did not slipped away. I could never show him how I could serve in ministry. This is a sad and even deplorable motivation for ministry, but it is the truth. Once he was gone, my drive went empty. The separation created by my father's death derailed me.

The second separation was the loss of my daughter Charity. Her illness and death occurred at a time when ministry and community service came together, and I was busy and productive. I was getting paid as a minister, and I was becoming well-known as a resourceful community leader. My wife and I had more money coming into the household than at any other time in our marriage.

When I think of Charity, I remember a young girl with a contagious laugh eating watermelon with friends, embodying the carefree light of youth. Charity was my buddy who hung with me for the last year of her life. She loved basketball as much as I did, and I cherish the memories I have of us at the Denver Nuggets games we attended together. We bonded in a way that I don't think we ever had before. Separation from Charity crushed and hurt me, and a sort of death penalty was issued into my life.

A large part of this crushing loss was my feeling that I needed to be strong for my wife as well as for the church where I served. They had embraced us and made her dear to themselves. I was trying to be superhuman during a time when even Superman would crumble.

Losing a child goes against everything we perceive to be right in life, and when you add my superficial version of valiant strength, you get a weak person. I tried to put my wife and the church on my back and carry them past this loss. In the meantime, I crumbled under the weight. I made poor decisions, and I pretended everything was all right. I failed everyone trying to be strong instead of turning toward God.

SEVENTEEN

Joy Takes Root

I had always been too broke and too busy to go to seminary after I got my bachelor's degree, but a seed had been planted by my pastor, Dr. Turner, who was one of the longest-serving professors at Duke University Divinity School. Looking over Duke's application and deadline one night after visiting in his office, I began to get excited about the future possibilities of studying at one of the nation's major seminaries. I was still broke, but if I were going to get in school that fall, I had forty days to submit my application, including a few writing assignments, copies of my transcripts, and reference letters. I completed it all, and after a few weeks in the spring of 2008, I received an acceptance letter from Duke. A year after moving to Durham, I saw my whole life changing, evolving.

Duke Divinity School made me do more than I imagined I would have to do. I wrote many thousands of words every week, from the first week to the last week of the program. Every writing assignment was scrutinized and marked for inaccuracies and needed clarifications. This writing rigor helps me today when I write a sermon every week. Because of the writing I had to do, I know I can write a sermon every week.

Additionally, Duke made me challenge every doctrine and theological position I held so I would be able to defend the principles I'd end up holding as truth. No longer could I say something was true without a thorough exploration of it; I had to look at its validity and sustainability through time. Duke made me better theologically than I was before.

Duke allowed me to serve as a ministerial intern in three rural United Methodist churches near Rougemont, North Carolina, called the Rougemont Charge, under the pastorate of Cheryl Lawrence. The Rougemont United Methodist Church, the New Bethel United Methodist Church, and the Union Grove United Methodist Church operated individually as churches but collectively to support a pastor and ministry. During the twelve months I served these congregations, I was able to run from church to church and had opportunities to preach regularly.

The three churches all had rural, White congregations. As a Black man, I was a change for them, and their being White congregations was a change for me. In my life, I had never spent time in rural churches, and I had only visited a few White congregations. For the most part, I believe they wanted to show that they were open to having a Black person in their pulpits, and I wanted to show that a Black person does good work from the pulpit.

One of the main differences between preaching to Black congregations and preaching to White congregations is that typically Black congregations will say "amen" when the preacher tells the truth. White congregations will typically look at the preacher and listen with no audible response to the truth. In the traditional Black Church, returning words from the congregation to the preacher are referred to as "call-and-response." One Sunday, I decided to teach these White congregations the traditional call-and-response done in Black churches.

I explained the basic rules to them. I told them that if I spoke a truth during my sermon, they should say either "amen," "preach," or "say it." Here I was in this rural White congregation that I had attended for months, having never heard one response during a sermon. Now I was challenging them to step into the outer limits of their imaginations by saying something out loud like "amen."

Before starting the sermon, I conducted a practice session by stating a few fundamental Christian truths that everyone would agree on. As I spoke a truth, I pointed at them to cue them to say amen, and they did. I started my sermon and preached for about a minute when I said something I believed was profoundly laden with gospel truth, and not a soul said amen. I paused and told them, "You were supposed to say amen right there." Amid their laughter, most of them said a loud "amen!"

I completed my sermon that day with sporadic amens sprinkled in from the congregation. As I stood near the main exit to the sanctuary, the congregants seemed to have extra smiles on their faces as I had taken them outside of their regular worship practices. One of the older women in the church smiled and said, "I don't think we are getting the hang of that amen thing." Pastor Cheryl Lawrence told me she would love to preach to a church saying amen regularly.

Durban, South Africa

During the summer of 2010, Duke sent me to Durban, South Africa, to serve in a large inner-city multicultural church. There, I came face-to-face with African culture in the post-apartheid era. When I had applied for the internship, the Duke faculty member who headed the program was Peter Storey. He had been Nelson Mandela's chaplain when Mandela was in prison on Robben Island, and he told me that he would only accept me into the program if I would go as a learner from the South Africans. I took that approach as I went across the ocean for the first time to Africa.

There was joy in South Africa, and I learned a lot from the people there. This same approach was helpful for all my future ministry work, especially when I started ministering to men in prison. The church I was assigned to was the Manning Road Methodist Church, where Roger Shultz was pastor. Manning Road had four worship services every Sunday. On my first Sunday, the Zulu minister and I preached all four services. Later that week, Roger told me that was the first Sunday in the 110-year history of the church that Blacks had preached all the sermons in the church.

I served at the Manning Road Methodist Church with another Duke Divinity School Student, Bonnie Scott. Roger surprised me on our first day, telling me that a family was leaving the country for eight weeks and turning their home over to Bonnie and me to live in. Bonnie, a young White woman in her midtwenties, and I, a Black man in my midfifties, were suddenly housemates, never having had more than polite conversations with each other once we learned we were going to the same church. When Roger informed me I would be sharing a house with Bonnie, I told him, "I guess it will work."

Roger told me, "You all better make it work because we don't have anywhere else for you to stay."

Bonnie and I *did* make it work, and we became close friends during our time in Durban. Yet we were indeed the odd couple in Durban. It was 2010—only sixteen years after apartheid had ended in South Africa. My observation was that Black men and White women did not often socialize and travel together in South Africa. Here we were sharing a house, grocery shopping, and driving around town together. Our age and racial differences elicited stares the many times we went places together.

On our last Sunday at Manning Road Methodist Church, Bonnie and I preached a sermon together titled "The Odd Couple" about how we were a strange duo like Jesus and the woman at the well. Ten years later, as pastors in two distanced churches, we brought our two congregations in the United States together during the pandemic and virtually preached that sermon again.

The Manning Road Methodist Church had one afternoon worship for its Zulu members, while its other three services were in English. I was informed that on my second Sunday there, I would be expected to preach for the Zulu service with an interpreter translating me line for line. Although it was not required, I went to their worship the first Sunday I was there to see what it was like. The Bible they used was in the African language of Xhosa, and though most of the Zulu worshipers spoke English, everything was spoken in African dialect once the service started.

I could not understand a word they were saying unless I heard them say "uYesu Kristu," which I believe means "Jesus Christ." While I could not understand their words, I could appreciate their worship. It moved and flowed like the Black Church in the United States. When the preacher preached, the call-and-response and spontaneous statements were just like the Black Church I knew. The regimented dress codes even reminded me of the Black Church's dress codes. Traditionally, in the Black Church, you are expected to wear your Sunday clothes, which is typically dressed-up attire. In the Zulu worship, the women dressed up in red-and-white uniforms. The men wore black-and-red dress suits, and the youth wore blue-and-white uniforms.

They did not use the piano, organ, guitars, or drums that the three other worship services used. Instead, some had leather pads to beat on to keep tempo, and others had a crudely made bell called an *intombi* made of metal construction pieces. A few of them would dance with the bell and tap it to create a ringing sound while they sang their songs. Their worship was not sophisticated, but it was genuine and never failed to touch my spirit. While I could not understand their words, I felt at home. I found myself going to their worship every Sunday, and I felt joy in worship that I had not expected.

On my last Sunday at Manning Road, I went to the Zulu worship, and they let me know I was the first student from Duke who had come to worship with them every week. They took up an offering for me in the amount of 200 rand, about thirty dollars of US money. I was so appreciative. They also gave me one of their *intombi* bells as an additional parting gift. My heart melted when they gave me that bell.

The Zulu worshipers at the Manning Road Methodist Church in Durban, South Africa, gather outside to thank Dewey Williams and bid him farewell after spending ten weeks with them.

The Zulu teenage girls play the *intombi* bell during their worship. The teenagers in the Zulu worship are called the Wesley Guild.

Graduating from Duke

I graduated from Duke Divinity School and started looking for work in the social work field and in ministry. I got jobs doing in-home family services with children demonstrating behavioral problems, and I did this kind of work for several years after graduation. I also started pursuing opportunities to pastor a church, something I had taken off my radar when I left Denver. I had suppressed my desire to pastor because I thought it was a source of tension in my life that I did not want to repeat.

Shortly after graduation, I had lined up four different churches to interview for. I was kind of excited about it because I knew I had gifts for the church through preaching, and now I had credentials from one of the top seminaries in the nation. I am not a preacher who relies on the standard Black preacher sensationalism of whooping with musical cadence at the end of a sermon. That was never my style. Many Black Baptist churches in North Carolina expect their preachers to perform with this style when they end their messages.

That is not me, so I always have a challenge presenting an exciting word that does not involve an end-of-sermon audible thrill. The Word of God itself provides the thrill.

I remember my first time sitting in a pulpit as a candidate to be the next pastor of one church. As I sat in the pulpit's biggest chair, the one the pastor usually sits in, I was suddenly overcome with emotions. I started thinking about being away from pastoring for the prior five years. I thought about fond dreams of pastoring that had slipped away with all the troubles in Denver. I'd thought I would never sit in the big chair as a pastor again. Tears welled in my eyes, and I needed to stop the flow before they ran down my cheeks. I am sure someone wondered, *Why is he crying?* I did not want to cry because I didn't think it was a good look for a pastoral candidate.

Neither that church nor any of the other three churches extended a call to me to be their pastor. Over the next six years, I applied to many churches in the Durham area and never found one that thought I was a good fit for them. I shifted my focus to doing prison ministry.

In 2011 the State of North Carolina closed the Guess Road Prison in Durham, and a sudden void was in my life. My outlet for preaching was gone, and the joy I got from giving and receiving from these men was gone. Richard Crandall, a member of Mount Level, must have seen an opening and invited me to be a part of Kairos at Central Prison in Raleigh. He told me the next session would be in August 2011, but a lot of work had to be done to prepare for a Kairos weekend.

Every volunteer had to attend four daylong training events in Raleigh in the weeks before Kairos Weekend. Richard volunteered to pick me up and transport me to these trainings and back home to Durham. Every volunteer had to bake twelve dozen homemade cookies to be given to those incarcerated in Central Prison. Richard assured me that he and his wife and other volunteers would bake the cookies for me. Every volunteer had to pay a registration of $175, and Richard told me not to worry about that either. Additionally, every volunteer had to write forty-two individual letters—one to each of the incarcerated men attending the Kairos Weekend. Richard also told me that the four-day weekends were long days but that the service done with those incarcerated was deeply meaningful.

With Richard providing the transportation, the cookies, and the registration money, many of the reasons that would prevent me from participating were removed. Richard was making a pathway for me to be a part of something he valued, and he hoped I would fit in with this ministry. I did the training with Richard, whom I found out was a leader in the Kairos work at Central Prison.

As I gathered with the other thirty or so volunteers going into Central Prison, there was a buzz in the visitor's station before we entered. We had trained for our visit, but now we were stepping into one of North Carolina's most secure prisons. We walked single file from the visitor's station to the prison's front door, then through the front door one by one. There we presented our identification and volunteer cards to a correctional officer. We had to leave all personal items in our cars, and we had to take off our shoes and walk through a metal detector as we made our way to the old gym. There, we would meet the incarcerated men chosen to be a part of this Kairos weekend.

As the volunteers walked from the elevators to the old gym, one of the men started singing the Christian song, "Surely the Presence of the Lord." His voice rang out against the cement walls and floors.

I could not see who started singing, but in a moment, all the men volunteering were singing.

We repeated the song several times as we made the walk to our destination, reminding ourselves that God was present everywhere—even in a place like a prison. I remember thinking the whole prison had to know we were there, because the acoustical reverberation off the walls had to be carrying the sound far beyond the immediate area. I will not tell you what happens during a Kairos weekend because Kairos likes those incarcerated not to know the full blessing until they are present. Hence, all I will say is that those incarcerated, along

Lynne and Dewey Williams enjoy a walk at Duke Gardens in Durham, North Carolina.

Dewey and Lynne Williams's daughter Tiffany with her husband, Christopher, and their daughters Isabella, Ivy, and India.

with myself, were deeply moved by what we experienced. Joy flowed from heart to heart during this weekend as well as during the other Kairos weekends I participated in.

During a Kairos weekend in August 2016, Jim Purvis, a Kairos regular, met with me and told me he and a few of the volunteers were doing something like Kairos with the men on Death Row. Jim informed me that Kairos did not have a ministry for Death Row, and his group felt called to reach out to this group of incarcerated men they had been doing Bible study with for years. Jim told me the group was called Short Journey. I told him I would join them in their October event and agreed to do a talk about forgiveness.

Years prior, I had resisted Lynne's desire to leave the house and city of Charity's death and to move to be near our other daughter, Tiffany, her husband, and the possibility of grandchildren in North

Carolina. My surrender to her desires was a key to me being in place for God's blessing where I found joy on Death Row. Today Lynne and I live about one mile from Tiffany, Chris, Isabella, Ivy, and India. We have family joy that we would not otherwise have had if we'd stayed in Denver.

EIGHTEEN

Joy Shared

A good preacher is supposed to tug at hearts, but on this particular visit to Death Row, I was sleep-deprived. My tired eyes gave in to the emotions tugging at my own heart.

The day before my preaching assignment on Death Row, I was extremely busy and finished my sermon late in the early Sunday hours. I had only two hours of sleep when I left home for Central Prison. Gratefully, Richard Crandall, my frequent driver to Death Row, picked me up and transported my weary soul to my preaching assignment.

My eyes strained to focus as I read my sermon. As I got to the story of Regina and Jeanne, I started revealing my emotions. I wiped tears from my eyes about the harsh realities of their story and the upcoming triumph their story would reveal.

Regina and Jeanne bonded against the will of the system. Regina had been kicked around from foster home to group home and back until one day she met Jeanne. Jeanne pursued all the legal steps for adoption but was denied because she was White and Regina was Black. The two were separated. Despite this setback, Regina used the words and inspiration Jeanne had instilled in her to attend college and form a successful business. The two reconnected as adults. Jeanne touched Regina because she simply wanted her in her life. The emphasis of this modern story is that God places people in our lives to inspire us on our journeys.

A prison is a place for tough men. Often in prisons, tears equal weakness. But the men on Death Row were also moved by the story and the fact that I shared a side of myself they had never seen.

There is a legacy of chaplains, social workers, and medical staff who treat those incarcerated as lowlife individuals not worthy of help because they are murderers of the worst sort. Many clerical chaplains work to get the men to confess to receive absolution before they die. Sister Helen Prejean outlined this approach in her classic book *Dead Man Walking* when an experienced chaplain explained the caution Prejean would need to practice in dealing with men on Death Row: "The chaplain says that 'these people,' I must remember, are the 'scum of the earth,' and that I must be very, very careful because they are all con men and will try to take advantage of me every way they can. 'You can't trust them,' he says emphatically. 'Your job is to help this fellow save his soul by receiving the sacraments of the church before he dies,' he says."[49]

For far too long there has been a passion in prison ministry to convince sinners to confess faith in Jesus Christ receive salvation for their souls. The problem with this approach is that it does not meet the incarcerated where they are as individuals. It further perpetuates the feeling that they are just numbers, insignificant souls yet to be saved. They are people with physical, emotional, psychological, and spiritual histories. They each have a story.

A better approach is to find commonality and relate the best we can. It's not easy. Most of us have not been accused of a capital crime. Most people can't imagine what it's like to live inside the most secluded section of a prison, even if they have seen it acted out on-screen. Most incarcerated people only have meaningful connections with family, friends, and other persons who are incarcerated. The women and men on Death Row who express joy are those who have learned to give and receive from the people God has placed in their lives.

The famed Jewish theologian Abraham Heschel wrote:

Man reaches a new vertical dimension, the dimension of the holy, when he grows beyond his self-interests, when that which is of interest to others becomes vital to him, and it is only in this dimension, in the understanding of its perennial validity, that the concert for other human beings and devotion to ideals may reach the degree of self-denial. Distant ends, religious, moral and artistic interests, may become as relevant to man as his concert for food.[50]

When circumstances hit us hard, we humans tend to isolate even though we know intuitively we do better when joined together. Dr. Vernon Bittner, psychotherapist and chaplain, wrote:

Another way we con ourselves is by believing that we can get along without other people. Maybe there have been times when we have been hurt by others, and we come to the conclusion that the way to avoid this is to steer clear of people. Many people are unlovable, vain, cruel, selfish, critical, and unsympathetic, but withdrawing from people is not the way to escape our need to make amends. The very fact that we are avoiding people probably means that we have not resolved some hurt or resentment.[51]

Writing prompt for those who are incarcerated:

Regina found a truth that is an enduring truth for all of us: God has a plan that involves us giving and receiving help from one another. I am here for you, and you are here for me. We are here for one another. You may think you are alone, but that is not God's plan for you. And it is not what God wants you to feel.

A Friend in Jesus

A common theme on this topic was shared by Fernando Garcia. He wrote, "God does not want anyone to be alone. That is why He said, 'it is not good that man should be alone'" (see fig. 18.1). The creation story impressed Fernando to make his case of how connecting

Yes I believe this statement is true? There is power and strength in numbers. God does not want anyone to be alone. That is why He said, "it is not good that man should be alone." And God created woman (a helper), for man. And when Jesus left to go to the father after His death. He sent the Comforter to be with us. So that we may not be alone. When one has a person to talk to, or to lean on. One can establish a bond, a true friendship, A fellowship that helps a person to become accountable for their actions. To strengthen eachother, to lift one another

Story:
ITS hard to write this one, because
I grow-up the only child. So I was always
alone while mom went to work. So all of this
transcended from my childhood to Now? I
Really don't talk to anyone about my "Noes"
I just take my problems to God, I am not trying
to give a correct answer. I just have a hard-
time talking and opening-up to others,
I do thank God that He is alway there
ready and willing to listen and to give
advice and to guide me. Because me
alone I am blind and lost. But I
have a friend in Jesus wants to share
a friendship with me. And I at most of
the times have trouble with that. I
con't at times iknow how to handle
that. That is probably why I have a
pretty good prayer life because I need
to know God before I give myself
and submit to Him. But thank God
He is always seeking me and willing
to help me even though I have many faults
an imperfection. Though I am on death
Row God shares His life with me.

Figure 18.1. Response from Fernando Garcia

to others is needed. He continued, "He sent the Comforter to be
with us." Fernando revealed his belief of how the Father, Jesus, and
the Holy Spirit modeled how much we need one another. As mentioned earlier, Fernando was indicted for the attempted rape and
murder of a young woman in her apartment complex clubhouse. I

invite you to read his testimony of how shared joy impacted his life on Death Row.

Fernando realized the need for others for accountability. He also contended that the best way to show you need someone is through shared activities upholding character and community responsibility. This accountability includes being honest with oneself and one's neighbors.

Fernando also grasped how connecting with others helps to avoid isolation, yet he indicated his difficulty in this. He indicated his difficulty in this. As a loner, he tends to stay to himself. Many people are introverted, and the concept of engaging with others is foreign or uncomfortable. Fernando's feelings created a dilemma for him because he intellectually knew the importance of finding connections, but it was not simple for him to make them.

Time Is Important

Iziah Barden, a barber on Death Row, shared the notion that God uses one person to help another to reach divine outcomes. He continued with a story: "When I started job of cutting hair on death row, I did not have a watch. Time is important. One guy give me a watch free of charge, some ten years later he ask to give me a new one, one week before the old watch died-out. I believe God move him to do so. God is good" (see fig. 18.2). This story seems so simple, but it is profound because it reveals God in the connecting. We just have to accept God's provisions when God sends them. Iziah felt this connection, and it was meaningful to him.

Iziah was indicted for robbing and murdering a coworker. He eventually confessed. His own words detail how shared joy transformed him.

> I think this statement is true.
> just like in one of my story.
> God use one to help another.
> and that open you up to get
> help when you need it. and to
> be more of a part of God's
> will. and a servent of God.
>
> story
>
> when I started job of cutting
> hair on death row, I did not have
> a watch. time is important. one
> Guy. give me a watch free of
> charge, some ten years later he
> ask to give me a new one, one week
> before the old watch died-out. I
> believe God move him to do so.
> God is good.

Figure 18.2. Response from Iziah Barden

The Load Always Gets Lighter

Keith East understood how sharing with someone during hard times can reduce the strain. He had his mother phone the mother of another incarcerated man to pray. This was what friendship meant to him. His act illustrates how much one man on Death Row can care about another man on Death Row. His poignant story of finding a way to connect with a nonbelieving man on Death Row showed his resourcefulness and that of the God we serve (see fig. 18.3).

Keith East often spoke about his giftedness as a young singer and how he was a teen prodigy with strong vocal skills. His life turned off-key when he was indicted for murdering his uncle and aunt in 1994. As of this writing, Keith helps lead singing in the weekly worship on Death Row—as if he's trying to tune his life in a giving way.

True, The statment is true for me
Because God's word tells me tha we
Are not ment to be Alone Adam Had
Eve And so on even at the worst
of times If you Have some one to
share your thoughts And Burdens with
the load Always gets lighter.
Story I Have a friend who is not A believer
But who's mother is, I often get on Him
About How God is Real And He needs
to understand what its like to Have Him
In your life. He Has A problem child
A daughter, Drugs, Booze, Running wild
He often comes to me saying you Have
A Girl what would or did you do when
she was 16, 18, 21, ect My Response
often vary But most of All pray I even
went so far As to Have my mom call
His mom And pray over the Phone
together Friends

Figure 18.3. Response from Keith East

You're Not Alone

John "Mac" McNeill believed that since God is there for us, we ought to be there for one another out of Christian duty. He wrote, "I know at time we think we are alone when it seem if no one care . . . but we are never alone" (see fig. 18.4). He expressed

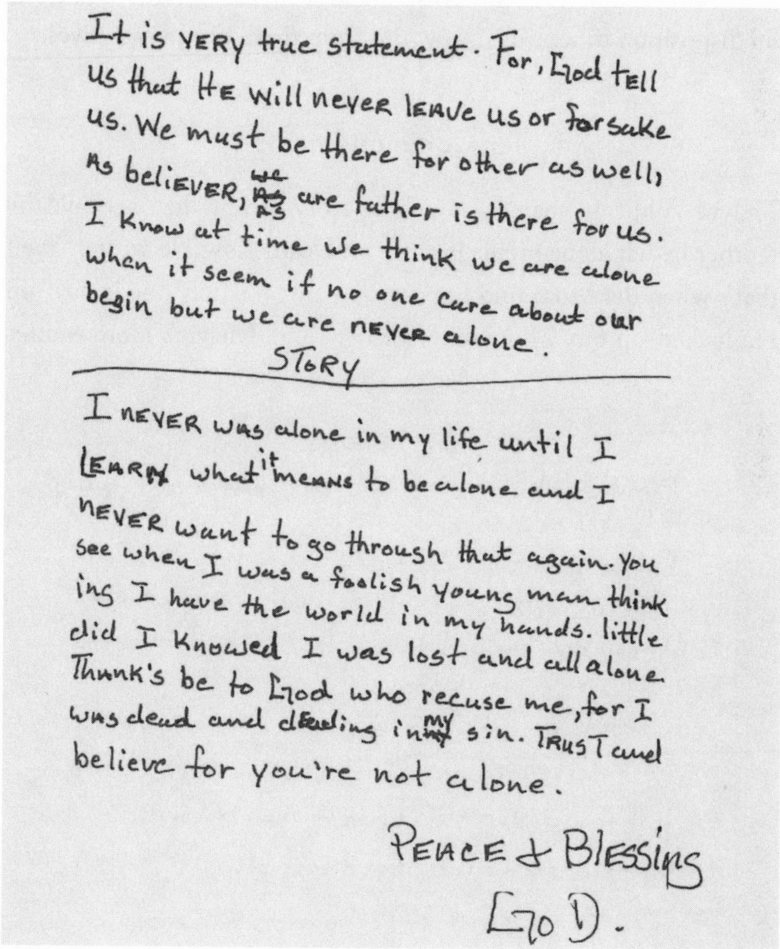

It is VERY true statement. For, God tell us that HE will never leave us or forsake us. We must be there for other as well, As believer, we are father is there for us. I know at time we think we are alone when it seem if no one care about our begin but we are never alone.

STORY

I never was alone in my life until I learn what it means to be alone and I never want to go through that again. You see when I was a foolish young man thinking I have the world in my hands. little did I knowed I was lost and all alone. Thank's be to God who recuse me, for I was dead and dealing in my sin. Trust and believe for you're not alone.

PEACE & Blessins
GOD.

Figure 18.4. Response from John "Mac" McNeill

gratitude for God's salvation and encouraged others to realize they are not alone either.

As previously written, Mac was indicted for first-degree burglary and first-degree murder of a woman he had been dating. The allegation indicated that his offenses took place in front of her two young sons, ages eleven and thirteen.

Mac brought a joyous smile to the worship services and a thoughtful disposition to writing. I saw him from these two perspectives.

Ten Commandments

Melvin White Jr. shared a touching story of how he once told his mother he felt alone on his journey on Death Row. He wrote: "Well, that's when my Mom told me 'boy you ain't the only one locked-up, I'm locked-up too, I hurt too" (see fig. 18.5). Melvin's mom wanted

Yes, God's plan for you/us, humans, God doesn't want us to feel or be alone.

In the begaining when ADam was alone God said to him it's not good for man to be alone. Even so that was for Adam to have a wife I believe that exstend to friendship.

(10)

The commandments that God gave Moses, they were to goven the relationship (first 4) between God & man the last 6 between man & man (humans's humans).

We need each other and the bible gives many examples. Life is not to be by one's self.

Story

Being here in prison/death row, sometimes I get the feeling that I'm in this alone, by myself.

Every two weeks (God willing), my Mom comes and visit me, we talk and share. On one of those visits I was not in a good mood and I said one of the most foolish statements, I'm in this alone. Well, that's when my Mom told me "boy you ain't the only one locked-up, I'm locked-up too, I hurt too.

My life, All of our lives effect someone, good or bad. We are not living alone, people are always think or praying for us. Mom, Sister, brother maybe friends.

Figure 18.5. Response from Melvin White Jr.

him to know that some of his pain was transferred to her. She also wanted him to know that she was with him on his journey.

Melvin Lee White Jr. was said to have a violent relationship with his girlfriend. The State's case was that Melvin killed two people in retaliation for his girlfriend's rejection of him. As previously mentioned, Melvin has vigorously and repeatedly denied the State's claims.

One Out of a Million

William Eugene Robinson, convicted of first-degree murder and first-degree attempted murder in 2006, indicated how having the right person in your life is like going against the odds. He used this gambling metaphor to show how God provides, even in times of adversity. From reading about his cousin, whom he called "1/ out of a million," we understand she was the Powerball winning ticket who helped him find the strength and courage to endure Death Row (see fig. 18.6).

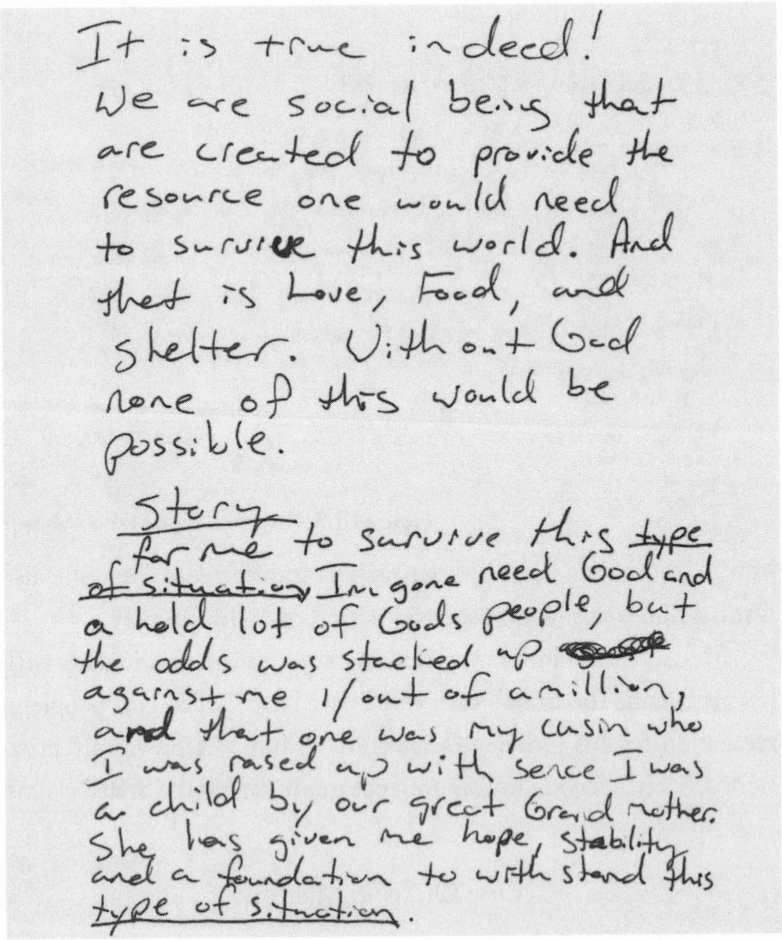

It is true indeed!
We are social being that are created to provide the resource one would need to survive this world. And that is Love, Food, and shelter. Vithout God none of this would be possible.

Story
for me to survive this type of situation I'm gone need God and a hold lot of Gods people, but the odds was stacked up against me 1/out of a million, and that one was my cusin who I was rased up with sence I was a child by our great Grand mother. She has given me hope, stability and a foundation to with stand this type of situation.

Figure 18.6. Response from William Eugene Robinson

Persistence

You may recall my earlier telling of how a man I met told me he was living on "Life Row." William C. Gregory was that man, and his words shined a light into my weary soul on my first day of serving with Short Journey on Death Row. God used him to tell me I was

Yes, I think this is True! For the first ~~four~~ years I believed I was alone. That God was absent in my life. That God didn't care about me or my well being. And I was one attending church here on deathrow. But little by little God brought two Christian people into my life and why became my God-parents. They showed me love and sincere affection. They brought God's warm embrace and realness to me in this dark, murky place were it felt like I was drowning! Ten years later God provided a spiritual Mother to me! Another wonderful blessing of God's providence upon my life. I wrote a poem called "God does not forget". Even on deathrow I know without a shadow of doubt that I'm not alone!

STORY

Someone said to me after I got a new trial and came back to deathrow to "not give up on God". That saying

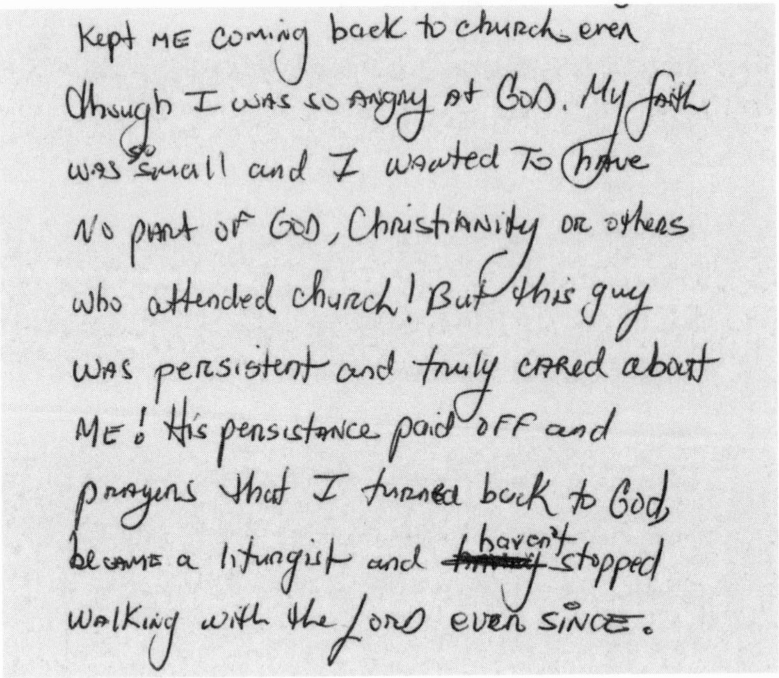

Kept ME coming back to church even though I was so angry at God. My faith was small and I wanted to (have No part of God, Christianity or others who attended church! But this guy was persistent and truly cared about ME! His persistance paid off and prayers that I turned back to God, became a liturgist and haven't stopped walking with the Lord even since.

Figure 18.7. Response from William C. Gregory

not alone and that my pity party was unwarranted. William illuminated my spirit in 2016. I invite you to read his words as he declared he was not alone (see fig. 18.7).

In his writings, William exposed his heart by revealing that upon coming to Death Row he blamed God. But God introduced the right people into his life, bringing a better sense of what God could do in and through him. He wrote, "But little by little God brought two Christian people into my life and they became my Godparents. They showed me love and sincere affection. They brought God's warm embrace and realness to me in this dark, murky place were it felt like I was drowning!"

He continued to write that even when he was angry, he knew he needed the encirclement of Christian fellowship. William told everyone not to give up on God.

The People God Provides

My personal story reveals that God placed many people in my life who gave me help. I also know I have given help to many. In my young adult life, I tried to present as self-sufficient, as one who was competent to manage my life. My presentation failed repeatedly. That is because self-sufficiency is a fallacious concept. No human is meant to live alone or to thrive by oneself. My competence and everyone's competence or success is only possible when it is connected to and supported by others.

My wife, Lynne, gives me words of encouragement and some-times words of caution. She is God's continuing voice in my spirit. My daughter Tiffany is passionate about many community matters. Our conversations are dear to me. She and I align on most social issues, and I enjoy spending time with her because she cares with a big heart for a better world. My son-in-law, Chris, is always ready when and if I need him. My three granddaughters are young, but God uses them to speak into my life every week. They do not realize they are imparting a blessing to me, but they are.

There are so many more people who share joy with me. God has placed in my life all that I need in these people. More than money or possessions, jobs or awards, I need the people whom God provides. I know that I am not alone. Neither are you.

NINETEEN

Joy Blossoms

In the spring of 2017, Patrick Clay, another associate minister at Mount Level, was the one who called me and said, "There's a church called Mount Bright Missionary Baptist Church looking for a pastor. You ought to go up, check it out, and submit your résumé." The church did not have a website, but I found some history showing that it was formed by formerly enslaved persons the year slavery ended in the United States. This told me that Mount Bright was a historic congregation. On a March Sunday morning, I drove over to Hillsborough to worship with them.

Driving into the parking lot, the church had a beautiful structure with a spiraling steeple pointing toward the heavens and a pristine lawn that gave the church excellent curb appeal. I entered the sanctuary and was greeted by the most cheerful usher in the world. Later I learned her name was Elaine Bellamy. With a smile, she said, "Welcome to Mount Bright. We're glad you're here." She knew I was a visitor because she had never seen me before. She handed me a visitor's card and invited me to fill it out. She spoke with gentle warmth. I would have been a sour soul not to fill that card out.

Their sanctuary looked like it could seat over 200, but the attendance was probably about forty. I was moved when their morning prayer was lifted up by one of their deacons, Walter Faribault. He prayed about the concerns of the congregation, but at the end of his prayer, he said, "Lord, You know what we need. Please send us the pastor that will lead us the way You want us led." His prayer matched the prayer that I had prayed: *Lord, if it is Your will, place me in a church.*

Mount Bright appeared to be a church that needed leadership, and I was a preacher with experience and training. I left their worship and decided to mail them my résumé for consideration. In June 2017, Eddie Eubanks, the chair of deacons at Mount Bright, called me and indicated that their pastoral search committee wanted to meet with me. I drove to Hillsborough for yet another meeting with yet another congregation's search committee. The meeting was cordial, and they seemed to like what I had to say. After that meeting, Eddie called me and said they wanted to schedule a time for me to teach Sunday school and preach the morning message. We set a date of August 9.

Lynne and I showed up, and I wanted to give them the best I could. Sunday school was in the sanctuary because they wanted as many members to attend as possible. I presented them with a typed lesson to show that I could produce written materials. The legendary preacher Gardner Taylor said that every preacher has a "candidate sermon" they preach when trying a potential new church. Well, I pulled out my candidate sermon, rang every bell, and blew every whistle I had. No whooping and hollering, just the solid gospel that was easy to follow and well organized. They loved my sermon.

Two weeks later, Eddie Eubanks called me and told me the church would have a business meeting to vote on whether they should call me to be their next pastor. I was expecting a phone call from Eddie the night of the meeting, but I did not get one. I started thinking, *Oh well, I guess I did not get it.* The following morning Eddie called me and said, "Pastor Williams, I wanted to be the first one to call you 'pastor from Mount Bright.'" I felt Mount Bright was a good fit for me and that I was a good fit for Mount Bright. In November, I started preaching regularly, and on the last Sunday in January 2018, I was installed as Mount Bright's pastor. Eleven years after I stepped down from pastoring in Denver, I was once again a pastor.

Unexpected Recognition

When given a chance to preach about joy on Death Row, I researched the topic by looking for scholars who have written about or spoken about joy. I always want to know what Willie James Jennings has to say on topics. He had been one of my divinity school professors at Duke, and his family belonged to Mount Level when they were in Durham. He is now a professor at Yale Divinity School. While looking for anything he might have written about joy, I came across the Theology of Joy and the Good Life project at the Yale Center for Faith & Culture. I was intrigued that a major seminary had a focus on joy.

As I mentioned at the beginning of this book, I discovered they were asking preachers to send in a series of sermons on joy and that they were having a sermon competition. I hated the notion of a competition because I do not like to see preachers vying against one another. Then I thought to myself, *I'm already engaged in a series of sermons on joy. Why not submit my sermons to Yale?*

I submitted my five sermons to Yale Divinity School, and I did not think I would have a chance of placing because their emphasis was on "the good life." I thought Death Row was not the angle they would want to project as the good life. But, lo and behold, I got an email from Angela Gorrell at Yale indicating that my sermons took first place. I was overjoyed because I have always thought that God gave me good sermon ideas. Now a leading divinity school confirmed that they thought my sermons were good.

A few weeks later, Angela Gorrell sent me another email asking if I would speak at Yale Divinity School's event as they culminated their three-year study on joy. If so, they would provide my transportation and cover all my expenses for the conference. I was shocked! I assumed she had accidentally switched my name and email in with the person they wanted to invite. Then it dawned on me that my sermons had won, which was why they wanted me to be there. I immediately called Lynne and shared the news with her. She must have felt the smile on my face through the phone call.

I responded to Angela and told her that I was available and would be glad to do it. She said they wanted something shorter than my recorded sermon, which was twenty-eight minutes long. Instead, I would have fifteen to twenty minutes. I agreed, thinking, *I am a professional. I know how to get a message across in a shorter time frame.*

Amazingly, a few weeks later, Angela emailed me and told me I actually would have a longer time slot and should not worry about keeping my presentation brief. I thought, *What in the world is happening? They want more of me.* That felt good. It always feels good when someone wants more of the good you offer. I felt my voice was desired and my ministry mattered. Once again, I called Lynne and told her the news, but as I spoke to her, I knew that what I would prepare would need to be a strong representation of what had happened to me on Death Row.

I decided to tell the conference at Yale my whole story, from Kairos Prison Ministry to eventually Death Row preaching. I decided to also tell them about the writings from Death Row.

I also wanted them to know that joy is so powerful that it creates a good life in a place designed to take lives. That was the message I wanted to share. No matter how dire circumstances may look or how bad events may become, joy is stronger than the worst we can face.

Lynne accompanied me on my trip to New Haven, Connecticut. Richard Crandall and his wife, Maggie, traveled from Durham to show moral support. Maggie, who had become my walking buddy every Thursday morning, said that she and Richard were the "Dewey Posse," always there to support. I was grateful to have people there who knew me and who I knew. Just like Death Row has preconceived stigmas, so does Yale. I was going to a place with a reputation for teaching and training some of the brightest minds and wealthiest

Dewey Williams speaking at the Yale Center for Faith and Culture at Yale Divinity School in 2018.

people. I came from meager settings where I barely graduated from high school, and my net worth did not require an accountant to figure out. Despite that, when I looked at the program for the first day of the conference, my name was in a spot typically designated for a closing session's keynote speaker. All the other speakers had time limitations throughout the day, but my segment did not.

Based on the seating and the number of tables in the room, there were approximately 225 people from around the world who had all made investments in joy in their work and lives. After I stood to speak, I gazed around the room for about ten seconds before starting. I panned from left to right and from right to left, taking in the moment, trying to lock it in my memory.

Then I started. I opened my deep baritone voice that had won a chance to sing in Bishop College's Concert Choir and sang:

> *Joyful, joyful, we adore Thee,*
> *God of glory, Lord of love;*
> *Hearts unfold like flowers before Thee,*
> *Opening to the sun above.*
> *Melt the clouds of sin and sadness,*
> *Drive the dark of doubt away;*
> *Giver of immortal gladness,*
> *Fill us with the light of day!*

I think Beethoven's music and Van Dyke's words were merged for a voice like mine. The conference was captivated with this song and my booming voice before I told them one thing about joy on Death Row.

I told them about my introduction to Central Prison through Kairos and how I preached on Death Row. I told them about my sermon series and how I treated the men on Death Row as if I were preaching at the most prestigious congregation in North Carolina. I told them how the preacher and those incarcerated on Death Row are kept at arm's length. There is usually a limited exchange between the preacher and the hearer following worship.

I told them what I thought was a miracle in going back and sitting with small groups and having them write about my sermons. I told them it was a miracle because the access I was given was rare, if not unique. I told about the strictness of the rules and how I felt all of Death Row was designed to strip away any chance of joy for those sentenced to die. Then I told them that joy superseded all that society had constructed to prevent these men from expecting joyous outcomes.

At this point, the audio/video staff projected samples of the men's writings onto screens in the room, and I emphasized some of their statements about joy. The conference attendees sat with their eyes fixed on the writings as if they were watching the pivotal point of a dramatic movie. It was like they wanted to know what the men on Death Row would say next. I thought, *They, like me, are finding joy through the words of the men incarcerated.*

The attendees of the conference were overwhelmingly White. I concluded my time by taking a risk when I told them I wanted to teach them a song about joy from the Black Church tradition. I asked them if they were willing to learn it, and I heard a loud united yes come from them. The song is called "Joy Bells." I sang the song that just repeats one phrase.

> *Joy bells keep ringing in my soul.*
> *Joy bells keep ringing in my soul.*
> *Joy bells, joy bells,*
> *Joy bells keep ringing in my soul.*

Then I asked them to stand to their feet and sing it with me. They gladly did and enjoyed themselves. I told them that when the Black Church sings this song, there is a little more emphasis that adds soul to the middle line that says, "Joy bells, joy bells." So we did it again but put some soul into that part of the song. When they sang that line, I told them to tilt their heads to one side and shake them a little on the word *joy*. They complied with my request, and it seemed they loved the song even more than they did at first.

While my sermons were good enough to win that competition, the best part of my submission was the handwritten responses of those who opened both their minds and souls and poured out of themselves how the messages of joy reached them in their maximum-security accommodations. While their bodies were locked away from the rest of the world, their writings informed us that this depressing milieu is a good place for joy to demonstrate its power to lift those in bad situations. I learned that joy goes to work in the direst of locations. I found joy on Death Row.

TWENTY

Joyous Reunion

It had been two years since I had been to Death Row because my new job pastoring kept me extremely busy. I missed those relationships and wanted to touch base with the men and women who had touched my life. I contacted the chaplains at Central Prison and the North Carolina Correctional Institution for Women. Both agreed to schedule two visits. The chaplains let me know that I probably would not be allowed access to them again for a year after that. I was happy that my visits were permitted, and I agreed to the restrictions. Chaplain Stratton and I planned the first gathering with all the men, realizing that we might miss some of them. We also planned a second gathering for those who missed the first.

A Return to Death Row

I met Chaplain Stratton at the front entrance, and we walked together through the prison's hallways to the final long hallway that inclined up to Death Row. For some reason, the chaplain had only prepared for six to eight men when I had emailed her a list of twenty-five. Then when she pulled up the list I had emailed her, she realized two tables would not be enough. I suggested that we have the meeting in POD 4, where all the Short Journey group sessions took place. She agreed, but this meant making some changes in that room, and she had to inform the correctional officers to change the meeting location.

As the chaplain and I walked to POD 4, we passed the door leading outside to a recreational area where the men get to go out for fresh air or play basketball. The chaplain said, "Some of the men may be out on the yard." A few minutes before ten o'clock in the morning, some of the men trickled in. Each one smiled as if glad to see me. I felt joy, appreciation, and love. One by one, they came over and shook my hand and engaged me in conversation. I had struggled to memorize all their names, but they all immediately knew mine and were glad to see me.

Since it had been two years since I last saw them, many of them asked about my church and how pastoring was working out. One of them asked if I was getting back in the preaching rotation on Death Row. It felt good to be in the presence of people who treasured me, thought highly of me, and were willing to let that be known.

Two of the men did not stay. Fernando Garcia was dressed in gym-type clothes and had sweat all in his shirt and on his brow. He said from the entrance of the POD, "I'm sorry, Dewey, I only get to go on the yard once a week for one hour. I cannot give up my hour for this. I'm sorry." He turned and walked out to go back to the yard. I was greatly disappointed because Fernando had written some powerful things in the previous times of sharing, and I wanted to encourage him in his writing abilities.

It got to be 10:15 a.m., and I suggested that we start because the men went to lunch around eleven o'clock every day. I began by telling the men I had not forgotten about them and all the steps I had been involved in to move the project forward. I told them I spent a year writing my life story that led me to Death Row and how meeting them led me to a better understanding and appreciation of joy. I told them I wanted to reproduce their writing in a book, and all of them agreed to sign releases, saying they wanted their stories told.

We were rushed, so we had to move quickly with the release forms and the four questions I wanted to ask them. This was somewhat disappointing because I wanted the men to take their time to write.

Pressley Peters, who was working with me to organize my thoughts, wondered if the men had had contact with any victims' families or had feelings or ideas about getting forgiveness from them. So I asked the men. According to George Wilkerson, they were not allowed to contact victims' families. George's comment reinforced a corruption that occurs in our criminal justice system—when prosecutors immediately create lines of separation between victims, perpetrators, and their respective families before a trial. Even after people have been convicted and sentenced to die, they are forbidden to have any contact with victims or their families. These are signs of vengeance and not steps toward healing.

Melvin White Jr. said with a snarly voice, "That question supposes we are guilty of the crimes we are in here for." I indicated that was why I never asked them to address that in their writing. Another man said, "Some of us are not guilty and do not deserve to be in here." Another man said, "That's right." I wanted to take time to deal with this issue and let them know that I believed some men incarcerated in the criminal justice system were not guilty. In this brief exchange, the three people who presented that they did not do the crime were Blacks, and I wanted them to know that misjustice is more likely to occur with Blacks than with Whites.

My mind went to the list of 186 people who have been exonerated after being placed on Death Row since 1973 in the United States. That averages over three people per year whom we have sentenced to die when our verdicts on their lives were wrong. At that moment I felt convicted as a coconspirator of the lie that takes innocent lives to death chambers. That evening at home I searched to see how many exonerations occurred in North Carolina. I found out the number stands at twelve. Of the twelve, ten were Blacks, one was Latinx, and one was White.

As the time neared eleven o'clock, I wrapped up the session by telling the men that they made a difference in my life. I had struggled with discontent, but meeting them at Short Journey, preaching to them, and sitting with them and discussing their writings moved me toward joy. I said, "Thanks for allowing me to share time with you, and thank you for sharing your thoughts and feelings on paper with me."

Then something happened that I did not expect. Spontaneously, several men (I wasn't counting how many) began to tell me how much I meant to them and how all I had done and was doing meant to them. They said things like, "What you are doing encourages me" and, "Don't be discouraged because you are doing good." One said, "I need to write to you." Another said, "What you are doing gives me hope." These expressions caught me off guard, and I was truly humbled. I bowed my head with my hands clasped under my chin. I looked up and said, "Thank you all for your kind words." One of the men said, "No, thank *you.*"

While shaking my hand, another man said, "I hope this is the last time I see you!" That caught me off guard, and he could tell I was perplexed. Then he said, "My case is scheduled for court review in the next few weeks, and I hope to be out of here soon." I told him I would pray for him and his case.

One man made an unusual statement I didn't know what to make of. He indicated that he and his girlfriend were getting married as soon as they had permission from the prison. Then he asked me to do the ceremony. The words that came out of my mouth indicated that we should coordinate all of this with the chaplain. The questions in my head, though, were: *Why would a woman marry a man on Death Row? Is this something that the prison system frowns upon? How does this happen when the men have minimal contact with people outside the prison? Will he be discouraged if this marriage does not take place?*

He was excited about this possibility of marriage, and I did not want to dampen his feelings with my questions. But this man's expectancy demonstrates how joy can be a strong driving factor in life. While prison walls and bars ruled this man's daily existence, the joy that came from sharing love with someone elevated his spirit into a blissful realm.

The men filed past me one by one and gave me a personal thank you. I have seen a volunteer kicked out of service because he was so overjoyed with the man's faith testimony that he instinctively gave the incarcerated man a Christian hug.

The feelings in the room were joyous because we all lingered together for several minutes—just like a church service that ends but the congregants hang around in the sanctuary mingling with one another. There is unique energy at church when people want to stay a little while and fellowship. On Death Row, this is different because when a preacher comes to preach on Sundays, the correctional officer directs the men to exit the room. They file by the preacher and exchange a brief greeting.

What happened during this reunion differed from all the other times I had preached a Sunday service on Death Row. There was more opportunity for fellowship between us all. Without a doubt, Christian fellowship can be a by-product of Christian joy, and without a doubt, fellowship was enjoyed that day.

This was the first time that the chaplain, Teresa Stratton, had seen me spend time with the men on Death Row since October 2016 during Short Journey. She is the senior chaplain serving all those incarcerated at Central Prison, and she oversees all the chaplains in this massive prison complex. And though I do not know for sure, I sense that she felt the connection between the men on Death Row and myself, and she felt that this project was encouraging for the men.

Reconnecting with the Women of Death Row

My first reunion with the women started early in the morning. I was scheduled to be there at 9:00 a.m., and the typical drive from Durham to Raleigh takes thirty-five to forty minutes. Since it was rush hour, I left at 7:30 to beat the traffic and get breakfast near the prison.

That morning I had prepared a basket of snacks for the meeting consisting of oranges, grapes, cookies from Dewey's Bakery in Winston-Salem, eight bags of Popcorners, a bottle of orange juice, and a bottle of apple juice. I felt this was plenty for the three women, Chaplain Prinn Deavens, and myself, but it was a handful from my car to the prison entrance. A vehicle maintenance staff member for the prison saw me laboring to carrying everything and invited me to put my basket on a dolly, and he delivered everything to the front gate. As we walked, he asked who the goodies were for, and I told him they were for the women on Death Row.

Once I reached the main entrance, I had to go through security to meet with Chaplain Deavens. She examined what was in my basket, as well as my large case, which held all my paperwork and ink pens for the women to write with. After that inspection was their screening. I had to take off my suit coat, hat, and belt and place my keys in a container just like at the airport. I walked through the metal detector, and the alarm went off. They sent me back, and when I went through the second time, the alarm went off again. They told me to take off my shoes. The third time the alarm did not go off. Following that, one of the officers patted me down, checking for contraband.

Chaplain Deavens met me and introduced me to Chaplain Key, who would be with me for the extent of the meeting. Chaplain Key had a wheeled basket for all my snacks, and we proceeded to walk outside from the security building to the building that houses the women on Death Row.

Once we arrived at the large metal door to the building, the chaplain pushed a doorbell, someone on the inside released the lock, and we went inside. We walked down a hallway until we came to a significant security guard station in the center of the building. There were five PODs in the building to house the women, although I only saw women in Section E, where Death Row for women was located. The correctional officer in the center of the building was elevated three or four feet above the rest of the floor, in an enclosed cement room with thick Plexiglas security windows. She asked the chaplain if we needed anything else, then excused herself from Section E by pushing a button signaling another officer to let her out. Suddenly the five of us were alone in the common area of Section E.

During our meeting, I was flooded with thoughts and emotions that one day the three women would be reduced to two women, and possibly to one woman if no other women are sent to be on Death Row. I worried about the bond these three women have and how hard it would be on them if one of them left or died. I had to bring my feelings up to the women. After the break I did so. The general assumption of the three of the women on Death Row was that if their numbers were reduced down to one woman remaining on Death Row, that one woman would be absorbed into a unit of women with special needs (medical, emotional, etc.) that are incarcerated.

We finished our time that day having the women address the role of forgiveness in their lives and what they wanted the world to know about joy. In total, the meeting lasted two hours and fifteen minutes, and the overall tone was joyous, with smiles and laughter as they told their stories. At one point, one of them asked me about my story and my family, which led me to speak about my daughter's death and how it had prompted Lynne and me to move to North Carolina to be near Tiffany. They seemed genuinely moved by my story.

We made plans for meeting in one week at lunchtime. That meant I would have to bring something more than snacks. Chaplain Deavens had come to carry me back to the front gate, and she recommended I bring Smithfield's Chicken next time. The women agreed that they would like that.

One week later, I returned to visit the women. Our time started at 11:00 a.m., and I was unsure what time they ate breakfast. I suggested that we could eat closer to noon if they had eaten breakfast late. They were not having any of that. They said they ate at five a.m. and were ready to eat. It was said, "No way we are going to sit here for an hour smelling that chicken." They told me they had not had fried chicken since the year before. As they talked, I thought about fried chicken being such a staple in my diet. My food options were a privilege that these women did not get to enjoy.

I'd brought fried chicken from Smithfield's Chicken 'N Bar-B-Q, along with some potato salad and hush puppies. I had also stopped at the store and picked up a couple of bottles of mixed fruit juice. The meal was topped off with some chocolate-chocolate chip and coffee crumb muffins. I could tell this meal was a treat for them.

After our meal, we cleaned up the table. Then I read one of my sermons I'd preached to the men on Death Row in February 2017. The sermon's title was "Miraculous Joy"—the one about Jesus turning water into wine at the wedding in Cana of Galilee. A closing focus of the message was that Jesus's disciples were instrumental in completing the miracle.

After Jesus's mother told the disciples to listen to her son, the disciples followed His instructions to fill the enormous water jars. Likewise, I noted, all followers of Jesus have a role in the miracles that Jesus will perform currently. I suggested that they, as incarcerated women in a secured setting, were disciples of Jesus, and that they must make themselves available to the commands of Christ to see the miracles that God wanted in their lives.

I asked the women to write about their interdependence on each other. After they spent about eight minutes writing, they read or recited their words about how their interdependence played a role in their existence as three distinct women on Death Row.

As each woman told of how they depended on each other, tears flowed down some cheeks. We felt the seriousness of the moment. After some silence from the discussion, the session ended with the women writing about their Christian transformation and the power of God to change their lives.

Coming Full Circle

The last of my reunion visits was at Central Prison. This session started with the hope of seeing the seven men I had not seen on the previous visit. Duke Divinity School had assigned a student intern, Tarvick Linder, to work with me while finishing his master of divinity degree. He accompanied me to this session, as I wanted Tarvick to have a once-in-a-lifetime learning experience—a rare look at a place that few people get to go and few in ministry get to serve. It took some finagling to get him in, but it finally came together. I felt an element of pride because I played a role in providing a unique learning experience for a student.

When Tarvick and I arrived in the Death Row community room where the session would occur, there were two long tables set up side by side, with enough seating for eight to sit around. Tarvick helped me set out pens and writing paper for the men, plus a release form for each man to sign. I was anxiously anticipating talking to William C. Gregory and Fernando Garcia. William was accidentally left off the list from the first visit, and Fernando had not wanted to miss his time outside. Both men had said and written good things in the past. It meant a lot to me to tell these men thank you.

As it turned out, the only one to show up to the session was William. One man had a scheduled attorney meeting. Another man had to work in the Death Row barbershop. One man had another detail to perform and said he would come in later if he finished. Another man sent a message that he did not want to participate. I was told that Fernando was taking a shower and would be there shortly, but he never arrived in the community room.

When William arrived, I told him he had written something about the game of chess and how it related to Death Row. I asked him if he could go back to his POD and retrieve it and ask the correctional officer to make a copy of it for me. He left and returned with the document, as well as a second document he had written. I was a little flabbergasted that both documents were typed because I understood the men did not have access to computers or typewriters. I asked William to help me understand. He indicated that one of the volunteers who came to Bible study typed and printed them.

Even after William took the time to get his writings and have them copied, he was the only one who had arrived for the session. I was disappointed because I wanted to see all the men, get all the releases signed, and show Tarvick a more significant representation of the Death Row population than just one man. I sat at the table with William as Tarvick sat in a corner taking notes. It was exceptionally cold in the community room that day. I had worn a long-sleeved shirt but wished I had worn a jacket. I am hypocalcemic with a low tolerance for cold temperatures. As I engaged with William, my energy was up, and the cold did not bother me at first. But the cold truly started to bother me as we got to the end of the session. My hands and feet are hard to warm up once they get cold.

I initiated small talk with William as I remembered some of his stories. I asked about his mom and stepdad, recalling that his stepdad was a church pastor. William asked how things were with me, as he remembered that I had been called to pastor a congregation when I stopped preaching on Death Row. I became fascinated with the idea of having this one-on-one conversation with the one man on Death Row who was instrumental in joy's transformation in my life. As we were carrying on our cordial conversation, I had a sensation or perhaps a revelation or maybe an inspiration that this may be a time to go more in-depth with William about his story and inform him that he made a big difference in my life.

I started probing him about his story by telling him that in 2016 at Short Journey, he had told me that he was not on Death Row but on "Life Row." It was William and me in conversation. Tarvick was almost oblivious to us as we talked. I told William that his statement "knocked my shoes off and stopped me in my tracks." I explained to him that I was in depression about my status in life and that his comments hit at the heart of my soured and complaining spirit.

I went on to tell him that in that season of my life, I was disappointed in where I was in life as a minister. I had always seen ministry as a service to others, but I had envisioned an income that would support my family out of that service. But instead of ministry supporting my family, the ministry was financially costly to me. Even serving as a volunteer in Short Journey came with its costs, as I had to drive to Raleigh for the training and for the sessions. I even had to take time off my job.

But perhaps even more than that, I was complaining internally that what I desired to see happen regarding my place in ministry was invisible. I felt lost to the world. Theologically, I knew God knows all, so I could not say I was invisible to God. I thought I could not say out loud that I felt lost to God, so I would say to myself, *Perhaps God is teaching me not to be self-centered* or *God does not want me in ministry*. But really, I felt that God did not see me or care about me. The day William told me he was on Life Row, I was feeling estranged from my purpose regarding ministry.

I am certain that I portrayed myself as a competent clergy member of the Short Journey volunteers. I was seminary trained and brought a ton of experience to the event. Further, I was able to address issues that prison residents had on racial matters. Typically, I was the rare Black person who had volunteered. Incarcerated Black men frequently mentioned that the White volunteers didn't understand what Blacks had to deal with. The volunteers and the men on Death Row did not know all my internal struggles, and they probably saw my projection of a competent minister giving service to God and God's people.

William's words, I told him, challenged me to reexamine my way of thinking. If he could reframe his life to see something positive, I said, what was preventing me from doing the same thing? What William said to me was not just positive thinking. It was *transformational* thinking for me. I told him that I left Death Row that day, and for the next week, whenever I talked to anyone about my visit, I repeated his powerful words. I even posted it on Facebook, and many people liked it, loved it, or commented on it.

Since it had been over three years since William spoke into my life, I asked him to retell me his story. I informed him that I was thinking about making him a focus in my writing. I remember William telling me how he was depressed and that he experienced changes that refocused his spiritual walk at one point on Death Row. Could he walk me through this transformation?

William told me that a part of his journey on Death Row had been his good support system outside of prison. His mother had been pulling for him his whole life, and even after he came to Death Row, she was constantly coming from Mocksville, North Carolina—a two-hour drive—to see him. He said she would show up like clockwork unless she was sick. He also indicated that his stepfather came with her until they divorced in 2016. Additionally, an elderly couple from his mother's church made regular trips. William was eighteen when he committed his crimes, and he was twenty years old when he came to Death Row. When his parents and this older couple came to see him, they gave him hope.

William was challenging his Death Row conviction in court, and he believed he would prevail. He reported that he was taken off

Death Row for some time, but after a court date, he was returned to Death Row. I remember thinking, *There is some cruel and unusual punishment involved in taking people off Death Row, then putting them back on Death Row*. William indicated that after returning to Death Row, he became very depressed—so dejected, in fact, that he did not want to move.

He stopped participating in all events because of his depression. He didn't want to go to worship or be with other men on Death Row. He had attended worship service in the past, but no longer. He said another Death Row resident, Alden Harden, encouraged him to return to worship, but he initially refused. William indicated that his mother became very depressed also, and though she cried extensively every time she visited, she kept on coming to see him. It was painful for them both. Between his parents and the members of the church, he kept getting encouragement.

One good thing about being on Death Row, as opposed to being in prison's General Population, is getting ten automatic appeals to your court case. When you are in General Population, you do not automatically get that many. William said this meant that he had more chances to go before the appeals courts and argue for his sentence to be overturned.

Finally William started attending the Death Row worship again, as Alden would not stop hounding him to come out. This led him to Bible study. During this season, he asked to be a liturgist in the Sunday morning Death Row worship services, and following one worship, he decided to stop living in his depression. He decided instead to restructure his thinking—what I call "living under a new matrix." He would not allow the systems to define his residence. He reiterated what he had told me before—that he was no longer on Death Row but rather on Life Row.

When the elderly couple became too old to drive to Raleigh, one of William's fellow residents had a pen pal he wrote to. When she started making regular trips to visit him, it was as if she stepped in and took the place of the couple that had stopped.

I asked how he felt about possibly being a focus of the writing I was doing, and he said he was fine with it. I asked if he thought his mother would welcome me calling her to get her stories, and he indicated that he knew his mother would. He gave me her phone number and said she should be glad to talk with me.

I told William about my worry—that my reporting his story might damage the appeals cases he is due to have in the future. He said not to worry about it. He knew his appeals were about the death penalty not being the right sentence for his crime.

It grew so cold in the room that it was hard for me to stay focused. When we did finish, I rejoiced because I got to leave the cold room and the prison. Mostly, though, I rejoiced because I felt good about the time I'd spent with William, hearing more of his story and telling him how he impacted my life. As Tarvick and I drove back to Durham from Raleigh, we talked about how we perceived William to be a changed person. His story of going back and forth on Death Row and going from depression to joy was a powerful message.

When I got home I found myself calling William's mother, Shirley Grant. After a few conversations, I planned on making a trip to meet her in Mocksville. She lived in a modern senior-living apartment complex where you must be buzzed in the front door to have access. She tried to buzz me in from her room but could not get it to work, so she came to the front entrance to retrieve me. One of the first things Shirley said to me once we were in her apartment was, "Chris did not tell me you were Black. You sounded like a White man on the phone." I was a little surprised by this statement for two reasons. One, I didn't know who Chris was, and two, my ethnicity is something that is not typically questioned.

I said, "Chris?"

She saw my confusion and responded with, "Yes, my son Chris. His name is William Christopher Gregory. We call him Chris for his middle name, Christopher. His father was 'Big Chris' and he is Chris. We don't call him little Chris." For some reason, this made her chuckle, as if there were some family joke about not calling him little Chris.

Shirley showed me pictures of Chris from when he was a small child, then when he was a teenager, and then a couple of pictures from when he was in prison. I could tell she loved her son, and what sent him to Death Row had hurt her deep in her heart. I felt mostly that she wanted him to be able to move forward. She was a woman of Christian faith, and she spoke about trusting God in all she did and about looking to God for direction. She had a professional picture of Chris when he was eighteen, dressed in a suit and tie, that was in a glass frame sitting on a table between her sofa and love seat.

I plunged in by saying, "That must have been taken the year he committed murder." She nodded her head. I asked her what happened. How did he go from this respectful-looking young man to someone who had committed murder?

Shirley looked toward the ceiling and said, "I don't know all the answers. He and his girlfriend had a baby, and their relationship had been off and on since the baby was born. They had been fighting and arguing for quite a while when he understood her to say that she was going to take the baby, and that he would never see the baby again. Chris became angry and lost it. That's the best I can make of it."

**William Christopher Gregory, age eighteen, in a photo
that was taken a few months before his crimes.**

We sat quietly for a moment, then I told her, "Your son told me
he has hopes of an appeal that might get him off Death Row. What
do you know about that?"

"Chris's crime was a crime of passion, which do not often get the
death penalty. He had an attorney that got him off Death Row years
ago, then his next attorney was a sorry one who did nothing. Now he's
back on Death Row. The first attorney has taken up the case again."

Shirley added, "They offered to switch his sentence from death
to life without parole, but Chris refused that. If you get life without

parole, you stay in prison for the rest of your life. He wants another sentence. If he gets just plain life, he could get out of prison after twenty-five years. He has already done twenty-five years. That's what we are hoping for because we want him to come out and come home."

I asked Shirley about the depression she and her son had experienced. "We all were depressed," she said. "It was like our hope had been taken from us. I cried a lot when that happened. I still hurt about this, but God is seeing me through it all."

Shirley's expression of wanting Chris to come home reminded me of Lynden Harris's musical piece titled "Believe" from *A Good Boy*, about two mothers discussing their sons who are on Death Row.

I asked Shirley, "What do you want everyone to know about Chris?"

She smiled and said, "He is the most encouraging person. Every time I go see him, he lifts me up and helps me to refocus my attention toward God. He does this with everyone he encounters. He has several pen pals that he writes and encourages them from his cell." Shirley made me think of the time he first told me he was on Life Row. His Death Row cell had become his launching pad for Christian outreach.

As we ended our time together, I asked her about church, and she said she had not been going regularly because of COVID-19 isolation. I told her about the church I pastor and that perhaps some Sunday, she could visit us online since it is a long way from her home. She would be welcome, I said. We told each other we would stay in touch about her son.

As I drove back to Durham, I thought about some of the meaningful writing William had done in the past. I had asked William to write about joy and self-control. Here are his words:

December 10, 2017

*Joy—A cheerful calm delight and rejoicing in a particular circumstance. (Acts 16:24–25)

*Self-Control—Is essential to keep the passions of the mind, will, and emotions suppressed, allowing the Holy Spirit to rule our lives. (1 Corinthians 2:16)

For me, life here on Death Row has been one of the most horrifying experiences that I could have ever imagined! This place affects me on four levels: physical, mental, emotional, and spiritual. I've been here for twenty-three years, four months, and counting. This dismal state is my own doing from the bad choices I made at eighteen years old. A choice that had a tidal wave ripple effect that not only affected the victim's family but my family as well. Tremendous grief, pain, and suffering have been caused by my actions that I have to live with on a daily basis.

Physically, I came to this place as a young twenty-year-old man. I am now forty-three years old and starting to get gray hairs. My prime years wasted away! Day in and day out this place gets monotonous. The same old routine from sunup to sundown. I watch myself slowly deteriorate from all the cold steel and concrete here. With all the stress and constant anxiety of being under the death penalty, I have high blood pressure. And one of the hardest things to cope with is not being able to physically touch my family at visiting hours. I have to constantly look through wire glass with bars in the middle.

Mentally, it's a challenge every day to not give up hope! Being at the bottom of the barrel in the judicial system. I'm considered the worst of the worse! That stigma labeled on me makes it hard just to keep my head up. This place is designed to make you think you're not a human being anymore. I refuse to see myself as an animal and fall into that line of thinking.

Emotionally, I have better days than others which is a part of life. If it wasn't for loving family members coming to visit me and always writing encouraging letters, I would have probably thrown in the towel a long time ago. When a man feels like no one care for him, and no one loves him or is concerned about his well-being, it makes it much harder to keep putting one foot in front of the other. Some days it feels like I'm walking through miry clay trying to find solid ground to stand on. Depression and low self-esteem can set in when it feels like my situation isn't changing for the better. Makes me question myself: "Is it worth it to keep on fighting and not give up?" Family and pen pals play a huge part in my sanity and state of hope in this gloomy place.

Spiritually, I gave my life to Jesus Christ. My faith and trust in Him allow me to see my circumstances from a different perspective. I know that when I add God to the equation, then all things are possible. He lightens my load of burdens and gives me a sense of self-worth. God has shown me that I had too much pride and anger inside of me. That I needed to change my character, swallow my pride and way of thinking (Romans 12:2). That process of sanctification has enabled me to live life on Death Row with joy in my heart. In turn that has led me to have self-control over my actions. Thank God for His sweet Holy Spirit which empowers me to live righteously for God's kingdom.

Inside these walls, it's constant internal battle each day. Learning to deal with self and others in a positive manner. I thank God for people who see me not as a number or sub–human being that can be redeemable and contribute to society in a positive way. At times it feels like land field have it better than those on Death Row. At least the land fields have recyclable bins that they use to recycle items of materials that can be used again in society. On N.C. Death Row, the judicial system sees me as just a murderer who is not fit to live. Someone who is not even redeemable. A man who is not fit to put in general population much less back out in the society. I've been here for thirty-seven executions, and I wonder if a change will ever come when North Carolina will abolish the death penalty.

Even in the dark valley, I realized over the many years that I was never alone. For my Redeemer lives!!! And O' the joy that floods my soul!!!

"Part of being optimistic is keeping one's head pointed toward the sun and one's feet moving forward."
—Nelson Mandela

Live Well,
William C. Gregory

Each person on Death Row has a voice. Usually, the only obstacle to their expression is the proper venue. In saying that, I would like to thank Mr. Dewey Williams for granting us the proper venue.

The Certainty of Joy

The theologian and the scientist alike often become squeamish with expressions of certainty. As reliable as one can think and understand a concept or a topic, variables and circumstances frequently present a countering understanding. History is filled with those who stood in certainty to find later their positions dashed by new data or new revelations. To paraphrase the first-century naturalist Pliny the Elder, "The only certainty is that nothing is certain."

With such limiting thinking, we might fall prey to concepts that suggest we have nothing to rest our lives, our faith, and our hopes on. I am glad to say that this is not the case. Based on our experiences, we can have certainty that joy will occur. We have certainty based on all the days of our lives. Every day we live on the Earth, it will rotate around fully; and as sure as that rotation will place the brightness of the sun on the other side of the planet, the Earth's rotation will soon bring back the sun's rays and push the darkness of night away. We are certain of this because we have witnessed it repeatedly.

I get a cue from remembering the scripture record following Jesus's resurrection. Two men were walking on the road to Emmaus following Jesus's death, unaware of the resurrection of Jesus. They were discussing all that had happened regarding His death. Suddenly the risen Savior joined them in their walk, and they did not know it was Jesus. They told Him some women had gone to the tomb, said Jesus's body was missing, and said angels were proclaiming Jesus was alive. Then Jesus began to explain scriptures to them. As Jesus was about to leave them, the scriptures say their eyes were opened, and they declared, "Were not our hearts burning within us while he was talking to us on the road?" (Luke 24:32). That was a sense of joy. Later they went to the disciples and said with certainty, "The Lord has risen indeed!" (Luke 24:34).

Just as these post-resurrection followers had certainty, and based on my experimentation and experiences over the past years (really over my entire life), I am certain that joy always comes through even in the gloomiest of circumstances. I have seen it repeatedly in my life in my family and in my communities. Just as the Earth rotates the night's darkness out and brings back the shine and warmth of daytime, God will rotate the darkness of circumstance to the point where joy's light will beam in its own way into our lives. It is joy's certainties that keep me moving forward.

I'm certain that we are all supported and sustained by the unfailing certainties of God's joy. I'm certain that hours and days and weeks and years may pass where hearts will be pained by disappointment and failures, but joy will eventually rise to bring in hope and move us forward.

I'm certain that the evil in this world will continue to attempt to smite expectations of justice and righteousness, but joy will continue to swing its battle-ax of moral outrage, to stand when wrong tries to prevail.

I'm certain that the thorns and thistles and briar patches of big-otry and racism, sexism, and gender demeaning will continue to prick and pull, attempting to turn us away from a blessed garden, but joy will bring forth the rosebud of fairness and equity and impartiality that teaches people how to love the immigrant, push back against police violence, and treat everyone—Black and White, male and female, gay and straight—as a sister or a brother.

I'm certain that we, just like an expectant mother, will have joy in the end. I'm certain that a better life will have morning sickness and pregnancy's pains, fatigue, stretched bellies, swelling joints, and the trauma of labor. Still, the joy of holding the new life God provides will outweigh all the discomforts suffered before.

I'm certain that the clanging of police handcuffs, the hammering of the judge's gavel, the closing of prison gates, and the clashing of prison doors in the ears of men and women on Death Row will not sound louder than the joy bells that God brings into the lives of all who will open their spirit's ear to hear what God is saying to them.

I tell you, I am certain that if men and women on Death Row can discover joy, then you and I and all who are willing to listen can hear the sweet sound of joy bells ringing in our souls. I tell you, I'm certain!

RESOURCES

Visit www.FindingJoyOnDeathRow.org for additional resources, including transcriptions of the handwritten letters, book club discussion guides for your small groups, and access to the full sermons given on Death Row. You can also find contact information for Pastor Dewey Williams and learn more about special bulk discounts for your group or ministry.

ACKNOWLEDGMENTS

I must stop to say thank you to those who helped me get this book completed. First and foremost is my beloved wife, Lynne. She has lived through every step of my adult life and every step of me working on this project. She even accompanied me to Death Row for Christmas worship and helped with music for that occasion. Without a doubt, I relied on her support and advice. I thank my daughter Tiffany and son-in-law, Chris, who heard about every step forward and every delay too. They did not give up on supporting me. I must thank my parents, whose deaths I mention as great losses in my life. They not only fed me but also formed me from childhood and planted God's Spirit in my spirit. I am who I am because of them.

Thanks to Pressley Peters who first wrote about me for Yale Divinity School, then joined me in helping to formulate the essence of the book. She contributed with words, ideas, organizing, reaching out to publishers, creating a book proposal, and eventually finding a literary agent. I am grateful for her contribution. Leticia Gomez, my literary agent, walked me through this process of submitting my book proposal to publishers and landing one that fit. Thanks to Dexterity for believing in this effort and bringing it to reality.

I thank friends who took the time to advise me through the twists and turns of writing a book. Richard Crandall got me initiated with Kairos Prison Ministry at Central Prison. He transported me many times from Durham to Raleigh for training and to preach. Calculating his help would take a team of accountants. Maggie Crandall is not only my weekly walking buddy but also someone who listened to my imaginations about the book and made numerous recommendations toward seeing the project come to be.

To those who have taken the time to read drafts and portions of the book, including Dr. Deborah Boston, Dr. Virginia Cruz, Dr. Braxton Shelley, I say thank you. Several others took the time to read portions too. Dr. Mike Broadway of Shaw University Divinity School sat with me following a visit to the campus and made a key recommendation regarding my writing that helped shape the whole project. Dr. William C. Turner Jr., as my pastor, was always available to talk with me and offer needed advice. I thank all of you.

To my ministerial student interns from Duke University Divinity School, I say thank you. Tarvick Linder, Shawn Lipscomb, Gilbert Barney, Robert Jones, Emmanuel Tabb, Stephanie Cassell, and Bryan Bernard each read portions of my writings and offered suggestions to make the book better.

The timely contribution of Ruth McDaniel and the team at United Service Foundation, who supported this effort with a grant that helped me move the project forward when it seemed stuck, made a difference. I am very grateful.

I am also grateful to Mount Bright Missionary Baptist Church, where I serve as pastor, for giving me the room to serve while working on this project. They are the best. And I'm grateful to Mount Level Missionary Baptist Church, which got me started in prison ministry and accommodated me preaching a sermon that was recorded for my submission to Yale's Theology of Joy and the Good Life competition. Also, the Mount Level Community Haven accommodated the grant received. I am thankful for their help.

ACKNOWLEDGMENTS

I am thankful for the men and women on North Carolina's Death Row who took the time to both listen to my sermons and sit and share their hearts in response to the ideas in my sermons. They will never know how much joy they brought to my life. Chaplain Teresa Stratton and Chaplain Prinn Deavens each gave me access to those whose spiritual well-being they oversee. I hope my access served them well. I know it blessed my life. May they be blessed more than we were all blessed.

NOTES

1. Billy Graham, "Is There an Answer?" http://www.jesuschristonly.com /sermons/billy-graham/is-there-an-answer.html.
2. Saint Augustine, *Confessions*, trans. Henry Chadwick (1992; repr., New York: Oxford University Press, 2008), 22–23.
3. State v. McNeill, 485 S.E.2d 284 (1997), https://law.justia.com/cases /north-carolina/supreme-court/1997/484a95-0.html.
4. State v. White, no. 505A96 (1998), https://caselaw.findlaw.com/nc -supreme-court/1460130.html.
5. State v. Harden, 344 N.C. 542, 476 S.E.2d 658 (1996), https://law .justia.com/cases/north-carolina/supreme-court/1996/427a94-0.html.
6. State v. Garcia, 358 N.C. 382, 597 S.E.2d 724 (2004), https://case-law .vlex.com/vid/state-v-garcia-no-895208745.
7. The name Richard Warner is an alias.
8. State v. Barnes, 345 N.C. 184, 481 S.E.2d 44 (1997), https://case-law .vlex.com/vid/state-v-barnes-no-890654678.
9. State v. Wilkerson, 363 N.C. 382, 683 S.E.2d 174 (2009), https://case -law.vlex.com/vid/state-v-wilkerson-no-887507788.
10. C. S. Lewis, *Letters to Malcolm: Chiefly on Prayer* (New York: HarperOne, 1964), 125.
11. James H. Cone, *God of the Oppressed* (Maryknoll, NY: Orbis Books, 1997), 8.
12. "Death Row Roster," North Carolina Department of Public Safety, accessed June 15, 2022, https://www.ncdps.gov/adult-corrections /prisons/death-penalty/death-row-roster.
13. "North Carolina Population 2022," World Population Review, accessed June 15, 2022, http://worldpopulationreview.com/states/north-carolina -population/.

14. State v. Jaynes, 353 N.C. 534, 549 S.E.2d 179 (2001), https://case-law .vlex.com/vid/state-v-jaynes-no-886787977.

15. John Swinton, introduction to *Living Gently in a Violent World: The Prophetic Witness of Weakness*, by Stanley Hauerwas and Jean Vanier, 2nd ed. (Downers Grove, IL: InterVarsity Press, 2018), 12–13.

16. Giovanni Frazzetto, *Joy, Guilt, Anger, Love: What Neuroscience Can— and Can't—Tell Us About How We Feel* (New York: Penguin, 2014), 13.

17. Jim McCloskey, *When Truth Is All You Have* (New York: Anchor Books, 2021), 265–66.

18. Gary Chapman, *Anger: Taming a Powerful Emotion* (Chicago: Moody Publishers, 2015), 42.

19. Charles Dickens, *A Tale of Two Cities* (London: James Nisbet & Co., 1902), 3, https://www.google.com/books/edition/A_Tale_of_Two _Cities/5EIPAAAAQAAJ?hl=en&gbpv=1.

20. Bill Webb, "Baptist Pastor in Ministry Through 'Prompting of God,'" *Mason City Globe-Gazette*, November 25, 1955.

21. "Slain Minister's Services to Be Held on Wednesday," *Denver Post*, August 9, 1976.

22. "Denver Man Fatally Shot; Daughter Jailed as Suspect," *Denver Post*, August 7, 1976.

23. "Minister's Daughter Kills Him, Faces Murder Charge," *Jet Magazine*, September 2, 1976, 55.

24. Miriam Greenspan, *Healing Through the Dark Emotions: The Wisdom of Grief, Fear, and Despair* (Boston: Shambhala, 2004), 7–8.

25. Frazzetto, *Joy, Guilt, Anger, Love*, 206.

26. State of North Carolina v. Archie Lee Billings, 348 N.C. 169, 500 S.E.2d 423 (1998), https://case-law.vlex.com/vid/state-v-billings-no -895688931.

27. State of North Carolina v. Christopher Lunore Roseboro, 344 N.C. 364, 474 S.E.2d 314 (1996), https://law.justia.com/cases/north -carolina/supreme-court/1996/156a94-0.html.

28. State v. Miller, 357 N.C. 583, 588 S.E.2d 857 (2003), https://case-law .vlex.com/vid/state-v-miller-no-892243972.

29. Mycrimelibrary.com et al., "Stephen Buckner North Carolina Death Row," My Crime Library, June 5, 2021, https://mycrimelibrary.com /stephen-buckner-north-carolina-death-row/, 121.

30. Mycrimelibrary.com et al., "William Robinson North Carolina Death Row," My Crime Library, June 5, 2021, https://mycrimelibrary.com /william-robinson-north-carolina-death-row/, 123.

31. Sendhil Mullainathan and Eldar Shafir, *Scarcity: The New Science of Having Less and How It Defines Our Lives* (New York: Picador, 2013), 26.

32. State v. East, 345 N.C. 535, 481 S.E.2d 652 (1997), https://case-law .vlex.com/vid/state-v-east-no-890137667.

33. State v. Phillips, no. 48A08 (2011), https://caselaw.findlaw.com/nc -supreme-court/1571796.html.

34. YouTube (YouTube, 2018), https://www.youtube.com/watch?v=U8 26OxCzfbc, 138.

35. "Research Resources," Innocence Project, accessed June 15, 2022, https://innocenceproject.org/research-resources/.

36. "Costs," Death Penalty Information Center, accessed June 15, 2022, https://deathpenaltyinfo.org/policy-issues/costs.

37. State v. Hyatt, 355 N.C. 642, 566 S.E.2d 61 (2002), https://case-law .vlex.com/vid/state-v-hyatt-no-886971755.

38. Larry Crabb, *Connecting: Healing Ourselves and Our Relationships* (Nashville: W Publishing Group, 2005), 143–44.

39. Larry Crabb and Dan Allender, *Hope When You're Hurting: Answers to Four Questions Hurting People Ask* (Grand Rapids, MI: Zondervan, 1996), 181.

40. State v. Gregory, 340 N.C. 365, 459 S.E.2d 638 (1995), https://law .justia.com/cases/north-carolina/supreme-court/1995/232a93-0.html.

41. Donald G. Hanna, *Mastering Self: To Lead Self and Others* (Bloomington, IN: WestBow Press, 2016), 408.

42. State v. Barden, 356 N.C. 316, 572 S.E.2d 108 (2002), https://case-law .vlex.com/vid/state-v-barden-no-895666065.

43. Howard Thurman, *A Strange Freedom: The Best of Howard Thurman on Religious Experience and Public Life*, ed. Walter Earl Fluker and Catherine Tumber (Boston: Beacon Press, 1998), 100.

44. Tobias Brandner, *Beyond the Walls of Separation: Christian Faith and Ministry in Prison* (Eugene, OR: Cascade Books, 2014), 23.

45. Laura Magnani and Harmon L. Wray, *Beyond Prisons: A New Interfaith Paradigm for Our Failed Prison System* (Minneapolis: Fortress Press, 2006), 51.

46. State v. Gregory, no. 19A97 (1998), https://caselaw.findlaw.com/nc
-supreme-court/1118574.html.
47. James Samuel Logan, *Good Punishment? Christian Moral Practice and
U.S. Imprisonment* (Grand Rapids, MI: Wm. B. Eerdmans, 2008), 70.
48. MarKeva Gwendolyn Hill, *Womanism against Socially Constructed
Matriarchal Images: A Theoretical Model toward a Therapeutic Goal* (New
York: Palgrave MacMillan, 2012), 68.
49. Sister Helen Prejean, *Dead Man Walking: The Eyewitness Account of
the Death Penalty That Sparked a National Debate* (New York: Vintage
Books, 1993), 25.
50. Abraham J. Heschel, *Between God and Man: An Interpretation of
Judaism* (New York: Free Press, 1997), 110.
51. Vernon J. Bittner, *You Can Help with Your Healing: A Guide for
Recovering Wholeness in Body, Mind, and Spirit* (Eugene, OR: Wipf and
Stock, 1993), 95.

ABOUT THE AUTHOR

Dewey Williams is the pastor of Mount Bright Missionary Baptist Church in Hillsborough, North Carolina. He has both served churches and held social services positions in the Dallas, Denver, and Raleigh–Durham areas for more than 30 years. A past president of the Baptist Ministers' Conference of Metropolitan Denver, Williams has led numerous community and nonprofit initiatives and been involved in various prison ministry efforts, including Kairos and Shorter Journey, since 2008.

Williams holds a B.S. in social work from the Metropolitan State College of Denver, is a graduate of Duke University Divinity School, and is currently a doctoral student at the Samuel DeWitt Proctor School of Theology at Virginia Union University. He and his wife, Lynne, make their home in Durham, North Carolina. *Finding Joy on Death Row* is his first book.